Chasing Dreams

Ernie Tolin

authorHOUSE®

AuthorHouse™
1663 Liberty Drive
Bloomington, IN 47403
www.authorhouse.com
Phone: 1-800-839-8640

First published by AuthorHouse 2/24/2010

ISBN: 978-1-4490-8381-6 (e)
ISBN: 978-1-4490-8379-3 (sc)
ISBN: 978-1-4490-8380-9 (hc)

Library of Congress Control Number: 2010901486

Printed in the United States of America
Bloomington, Indiana

This book is printed on acid-free paper.

This book is dedicated to
My mentors Lisle Green
And Verdie White.

TABLE OF CONTENTS

INTRODUCTION

Over the years, I have been called the story teller. Perhaps, I got this title because I enjoy talking about my adventures with the U.S. Forest Service. I have always viewed my life as a series of adventures beginning with my earliest recollections and continuing all the way through the growing up years until my retirement.

My parents were both attorneys. My dad went on to become a United States Attorney. He tried some interesting cases including the successful prosecution of mobster Mickey Cohen. He later became a Federal Judge. In my younger years, my mother worked for the Immigration and Naturalization Service. She went on to become an assistant U.S. Attorney working in the Lands division. As fate would have it my mom tried several cases for the Forest Service including the Colman case which involved illegal trespass on Forest Service Lands. She also pursued the concept that if anyone damaged Forest Service Lands, they should be responsible for paying the cost of restoration.

As a teenager I became engrossed with working on cars and racing them at the San Gabriel and San Fernando Drag strips. In the 1950's the communities sponsored drag racing. In the Los Angeles area there were 3 drag strips where a person could enter his car in supervised drag races or just run his car on the quarter mile to see how fast his car could go.

As a youngster I had dreamed of going to Annapolis and getting a commission in the Navy. In my junior year of high school I found out that because I had less than perfect eyesight, that I would not be able to go to Annapolis. At that point I was lost and thought that I would spend the rest of my life being an automobile mechanic. How wrong I was! I would go on to enjoy an exciting life doing things that the average person never gets a chance to do.

To help me find myself, my dad took me to see a specialist who gave aptitude tests. I took a battery of tests and when the results came back, I was told that I had a knack for figuring out ways to streamline production or business systems. Later in my life, this forecast would come true.

Early Recollections

The earliest memory that I have is being lost, walking on a sandy beach, crying and looking for my mommy. I don't remember who found me but eventually someone saved me. Years later the same thing would happen to my youngest son.

I was born just before World War II. As a child of that era, I have several memories of living during war time where the outcome of the war would affect everyone's life in the world. As it was just being at war affected everyone's life. We were constantly reminded about the war as it was common to see the sky full of war planes flying in formation over our house. I remember looking up at the planes and wishing that I could fly in one of them. Little did I know that one day I would have the opportunity to fly in several different types of WWII aircraft. Some of my favorite toys were toy airplanes made of wood and in very rare instances metal. Plastic was not available in the early 1940s.

The house that we lived in had a small hall in the center of the house. This was the spot where my parents would go when there was a blackout. Blackout was the term that was used during the war for an air attack at night. The thought was that if the enemy couldn't see any lights, they would not know that they were over a populated area like Los Angeles.

During a blackout all lights that could be seen from outside the house had to be turned off. The only lights that could be on were ones located in places like our hallway. Enforcement of the lights out was done by air raid wardens. They would patrol the streets and if they saw a light on in your house, they would bang on the door and order you to turn the light off.

Other things that I remember was driving someplace in Los Angeles and seeing what looked to me like a very large tent. My dad told me that this was a form of camouflage. The intent was to fool enemy aircraft to think that they were flying over the country not a major downtown area of So. California. Another memory is that down near the Long Beach airport and some aircraft factories, you could see the entrances to air raid shelters. These entrances did not disappear until the early 1950's. My parents purchased a very nice home in Pasadena, California for about $5000.00. This was because of a panic following an enemy submarine that torpedoed a pier near Long Beach. At that early point, during the war the price of real estate in So. California got real cheap. There was a real fear that we were about to be invaded. It was in our house in Pasadena that we heard that the war ended. So did the rationing of certain food items and gasoline. During the war it was a real treat to get a candy bar and I remember one of our relatives who was in the Navy bringing us a box of candy bars. An item that you could not buy at any price was butter. Margarine, was the closest one could come to butter. The margarine was white and came with a color pack that you could use to color the margarine by mixing it with the color pack. It took a year or two following the war before you could purchase real butter. Because of the war effort production of automobiles stopped sometime in 1941. 1947 was the first time that you could purchase a new car. To do this you had to get on a long waiting list. My parents purchased a 1947 Studebaker. The body style of that make of car was the talk of the town. The reason was the extended trunk that the car had.

I remember starting pre school then moving on to kindergarten and one day about mid term, I decided that I did not want to go to school that day. This was one of the biggest mistakes of my life. My mom kept me in bed then took me to see a doctor. I was diagnosed as having rheumatic fever. I went through the 1st grade confined in my bed and finally got released to start school again. A few years later, we were told that I had never had rheumatic fever. The problem had been part of my body was growing faster than it should have.

By the ninth grade, my parents put me in a private school for boys to prepare me for taking the test and getting accepted into the Naval Academy. After a few months at the private school, I was put on probation and told that I needed to improve my grades or I would be expelled. Somehow, I managed to stick with it until graduation. By my junior year, I found out that my eyesight was not good enough for the Naval academy. What now ? As it turns out, I had become an accomplished mechanic working on cars, racing them so it seemed natural that I would become a mechanic. My dreams turned towards buying a gas station and opening a small garage. My parents were horrified at this idea.

Following high school graduation, I joined the army and enlisted in what was then called the six month plan. It called for six months of active duty, followed by 3 ½ years of ready reserve and four years of standby reserves. This decision ultimately saved my Forest Service career. The Berlin wall went up and many guys my age got drafted. Because I was in the reserves, the draft was not able to call me up.

Just before I left for my six month army tour, I met my wife to be. A friend of mine invited me to go to dinner with him and another friend. When we got to the restaurant my friend Chuck introduced me to his new girlfriend who he had met in summer school. Shortly after my return from the army I would begin dating this girl. Upon my return from six months active duty, I entered the local college, Pasadena City College (PCC). I dropped out after a few months and went to work in a small gas station / garage. I was very discouraged with college as I was being forced to take all those subjects that I had just completed in high school. Granted the courses were at college level but they were not teaching me anything new. I re enrolled in the fall and majored in auto mechanics. After a few months of dating the girl of my dreams, I got engaged and then got married in mid June. My parents were horrified, but since I was over 18, they went along with it.

I tried a couple of things before I got married. I tried working in a steel heat treating plant and then moved on to a brake bonding plant. I commanded an average salary of $1.50 per hour. My bride went to work as a shipping and receiving clerk and earned $1.40 per hour. In 1958 a couple could live on this. Rent was $80.00 per month food was about $10.00 per week and utilities were around $12.00 per month.

My dad helped me find a better job a few months after I got married. The job I got was working as a sheet metal apprentice for a company that manufactured ultraviolet lights and florescent paints. The company also built several displays for the new Walt Disney Land. Projects that I worked on included the submarine ride and Rainbow Caverns.

I had worked for the Ultraviolet company for about a year and had advanced in salary to almost $2.00 per hour. Note, the company didn't have any benefits. A friend of ours told me one day that he was leaving his job in the US Forest Service and he wanted to know if I would be interested in the job. The job involved working with fire fighting aircraft. I had always been interested in flying so I took him up on his offer. After a brief interview, I was hired and a new life began.

Forest Service in the Golden Days Philosophies

The Forest Service has changed a lot since I retired. In 1960 when I joined the outfit, the service was dedicated to serving the public and managing the Nations natural resources. The Forest Service is an agency in the Department of Agriculture. It is often confused with the US Park Service which is an agency in the Department of Interior. The news media often gets this confused. The Forest Service and the Park Service have distinct and different philosophies on land management. The Park service tends to let nature take its course. For example if there is a fire in a National Park the Park Service will generally let it burn and after the fire is out let nature take its course.

The Forest Service on the other hand manages its land. If there is a fire on National Forest land, every effort is made to put the fire out. The Forest Service views trees as crops and through careful management will harvest its crop of trees on a schedule. Often the crop is over 100 years old when is selected for harvest.

The Forest Service has changed since the golden years of the 1960's and 1970's. During those years, the agency was quite responsive to the public and its needs. In the Golden years the National Forest Systems more than paid for its operations. The fees collected from the sale of timber, lease of grazing lands, Special Use Permits etc. more than covered the operation of the National Forest System. The revenue generated from the Forest was sent to the US Treasury. The Forest Service was not allowed to spend the funds it took in. Operating money was appropriated by the US Congress. Operating funds were always a lot less than the revenue generated.

In today's environment the Forest Service is not nearly as responsive to the public as it was during the Golden years. Congress and the White House have forced the agency to consolidate and centralize many of the activities that once took place on the Ranger Districts and the Forest Supervisors Office. Things like personnel management, procurement and contracting have been moved into zones. It is no longer an acceptable practice for a student wanting summer work to walk into a District or Supervisors Office and apply for a job. Applications for seasonal work must be sent in during the month of December. The process is awkward and results in the agency not being able to fill many of its critical summer time positions. Now days, one can read about the personnel shortages in the Forest Service and the hiring of foreign non English speaking crews The explanation is that Americans do not want that kind of work. I know from personal experience that this is not true. During the Golden years someone always answered the phone and there were no answering machines. I had a recent experience where I left a message on a Directors answering machine and the call was returned about six months later.

My 1st Job

I was hired into the Forest Service as an Air Service Manager. The position was on the Angeles National Forest which is north of Los Angeles in the San Gabriel mountain range. I was classified as a labor II and made $2.50 an hour which in 1960 was not a bad wage. You could live on it. My first appointment was for 180 days and I was told that I would be laid off following fire season. Fire season ended after the first rain fall of at least 1 inch. In later years this would change and the season would end because congress would not appropriate enough funds to keep fire crews on until the threat of fires was diminished due to adequate rainfall. My long term goal was to get a permanent appointment that would keep me working year round. I also dreamed of one day becoming a GS 9 working out in the national forest. With my education a GS 9 would be about as far as I could go and I would be very lucky to get that far.

My view of all this was, that the job was like being a teacher. One would work until fire season ended then do something else until the new fire season started, generally in mid May. Workers who returned would usually get a permanent appointment after being rehired three years in a row.

Chino airport was where I was stationed and at the time I worked there, the TV series 12 O'clock High was being filmed there. To get to our control tower, we would drive through the movie set which was kind of eerie late at night or before sun rise. The set looked like what one would expect an army air force base to look like during World War II. Buildings were marked with signs like 918 Headquarters, Operations, etc.

On my first day at work, I reported in and was briefed on how the airport operated. With every flight and every fire there was a lot of paperwork. The time that each aircraft was in the air and the load of retardant that it carried had to be written up so that the owner of the aircraft could get paid. If an aircraft and pilot were designated initial attack, the plane could be dispatched to a fire without a Forest Service lead plane. Pilots who were rated initial attack had a great track record of hitting their target while pilots who frequently missed their targets had to be escorted to the drop site. Part of our job was to make sure that the ground crew that loaded the aircraft didn't inadvertently walk into the prop of an aircraft which had just landed or was getting ready to take off. You would think this would be simple, and that common sense would keep crew members away from spinning props, but with the excitement and the eagerness to get the planes loaded and back into the air, crewmen would forget about the hazards of aircraft with spinning props. The ground crew was made up of workers who worked for the airport fuel concession. If the fire lasted for more than a few hours, off duty volunteer workers from the Chino fire department would show up and load planes and mix borate.

In the early 1960s two types of retardant, Borate and Bentonite, were used. Borate was the most popular retardant and it was common to hear the term Borate bombers used. Borate is a mud that is used for cooling drilling bits on oil rigs. It sticks to vegetation and makes the vegetation fireproof. One small problem with borate is that it is a great soil sterilant

and for years following a fire, you could see where Borate and Bentonite had been dropped. Bentonite was also a mud that had the same primary use as borate. For identification purposes, Bentonite was dyed bright red while Borate retained a brown mud color.

During the 1st part of the fire season, borate was mixed using a glorified cement mixer and a couple of crewmen who would load the powder into the mixer, add water and when the mix was ready, pump it into a large storage tank. As the season progressed, the owner of the fueling concession automated the borate mixing process. This was done using a conveyer belt which would pass a bag of borate over a running table saw. When the bag left the saw table, it ran into a couple of spears at the ends of the bag. The spears would hold the end of the bag while the center of the bag would open up dropping the dry borate into a mixing hopper. This process was faster than the old system and was less labor intensive.

There were two Forest Service lead planes stationed at Chino. These were navy T34 B single engine aircraft. The T34 was a great stunt plane and had been used by the navy to train pilots as jet fighter pilots. The plane was a two seat aircraft with a clear canopy. A red arrow pointed to the cockpit and the word RESCUE was painted in black.

Contract aircraft assigned to Chino included a B17, two B25s, four torpedo bombers (TBMs), two navy PBYs, and a privateer. An interesting note is that the B25s were owned and operated by Paul Mantz who was in the movie making business. Paul was killed several years later while filming the movie "Flight of the Phonix". Air tankers were paid on an hourly basis for their work. The cheapest tanker at Chino was the TBM which made $600.00 per hour. The most expensive aircraft was the B17 which was paid $1000.00 per hour. B17's carried 2000 gallons of retardant while TBMs carried about 600 gallons of retardant. The B25s started the season carrying 1000 gallons of retardant but this was reduced to 800 gallons later in the season when it was determined that 1000 gallons was too much for a B25.

PBY Making a Drop

The 1960 fire season claimed 7 B25 aircraft. The problem was that when a retardant drop was made, the Gforce associated with the release of the retardant could do one of several things to the aircraft. In most cases nothing would happen but in other cases, the sudden lift would rip the wings off or flip the plane on its back causing the crew to lose control. Chino had other losses during the 1960 season. One was due to pilot error and the cause of other accident was never determined. It should be noted that when an air tanker goes down while fighting a fire, there are never any survivors.

The first day on the job went without any fires or incidents. On my 2nd day, my boss suggested that I go over to Ryan field in Hemet and meet my counterpart. I was given a white crash helmet with a built in headset and microphone and told to report to the flight line where a T34, 02 ZULU, was waiting with the pilot, Bob Clark. Bob opened the canopy for me and helped me get strapped into the 2nd seat. He showed me where to plug my headset in and how to activate it so I could talk to him. He also told me to keep my hands and feet off the controls. With this, he climbed up front and started the engine up. In 1960, Chino had a long and a short runway. We taxied to the short runway where Bob did all his pre flight checks. Once completed, the canopy was closed and we were off.

This was my first experience in riding in a small single engine aircraft. The take off was smooth and we climbed quickly to about 5000 feet. I was impressed. I looked forward at the altimeter and the other instruments. This was very close to a childhood dream of wanting to fly in a jet aircraft. Out of the clear blue, the plane began a very steep dive then leveled off. I knew we were very low as the left wing was level with the hood of a pickup truck that was facing us. After a couple of seconds, we nosed up and climbed back to our cruising altitude of 5000 feet. I got on the intercom and asked Bob what that was all about. He told me that he had just been shooting a landing at a very small private airfield. Soon Hemet Ryan field was in sight. Our T34 went into the approach pattern and began the descent. Soon a horn sounded inside the cockpit. I was told later that this was a stall warning that was telling us that the speed of the aircraft was reaching that point where the plane would no longer fly. The runway was under us and Bob cut power to the engine and eased back on the stick. The sensation was like we were floating on a cloud. The aircraft settled to the runway and we taxied over to the control tower and flight line.

I met my counterpart and he filled me in on how the two airports cooperated with one another during fire operations. I told him that I was just learning and asked him to be patient. Hemet Ryan airport is assigned to the San Bernardino National Forest. In 1960, the Forest Service was the only fire suppression agency on the airport. By 1980 the State of California Division of Forestry (CDF) was the predominant fire agency.

Following my meeting we returned to Chino and I knew that this flying thing was for me. A few days later, I was asked if I would like to take a ride in the B17. The crew was going out on a training flight and passengers were invited. What a novelty, being able to ride in an old World War II bomber. The B17 had a pilot, and a co pilot. There were a couple of extra chairs directly behind the pilots chair. We took off and flew down to Corona where we spent a lot of time doing figure eights. This was an experience as up until now, I had never experienced what a G force felt like. At the time, the B17 seemed to be a very large airplane. As we were doing the figure eights, I looked down the wing which seemed to be quite long. After about an hour's flight, we returned to Chino.

One hot afternoon just after lunch, our tower was rocked by a very loud boom. We looked at each other and then concluded that we had just been hit with a sonic boom. In the early days of super sonic aircraft we would experience a sonic boom two or three times a year. About a minute later, the forest radio network came alive. The call was from Sunset lookout. The person on duty that day was Sandy. Her transmission started out normally with her call sign to Arcadia dispatch. We heard "Arcadia Sunset Lookout". The dispatcher responded Arcadia. The radio was silent for several seconds then we could hear what sounded like somebody panting into their microphone. Finally Sandy screamed Fire and that was all she could say.

Dispatch quickly started calling other units near Sunset lookout to see if they had observed anything. A patrol on the Angeles Crest highway called in and reported a major fire that was very close to Sunset Lookout. In a matter of moments Arcadia Dispatch called us and gave us a distance and heading to the fire. The message said start the TBMs. We turned on the fire siren and the airport came alive. People appeared from nowhere. Pilots were running to their aircraft, crewmen were following standard procedure and loading the TBMs with retardant. The 1st TBM was loaded and the loading crew moved to the second TBM in the line. While all this was going on, the lead plane 02 ZULU was taxiing out and getting ready for take off. We radioed 02 giving him the bearing and miles to the fire. Shortly after, we cleared the 1st TBM for take off. This whole drill took less than 5 minutes to get the lead plane in the air and the 1st TBM taxiing down the taxi way for take off. As per our standard operating procedures, the 3 available TBMs would be spaced about 5 minutes apart for take off. This approach was used to minimize the amount of time that the aircraft would need to orbit the fire until the lead plane could take the tanker into the drop zone. Procedures for the lead plane to guide a plane to the drop zone were for the lead plane pilot to instruct the air tanker pilot to follow him. When the lead plane got over the drop zone, the lead plane would rock its wings back and forth. The lead plane and the tanker would then go around and the lead plane would follow the tanker to the drop site. Once in position, the tanker would drop his load of retardant. The lead plane would record whether the drop had hit or missed the target.

Back at Chino the order was given to start the remaining aircraft. The PBYs were loaded and launched, followed by the B25s and the B17. Last but not least, the privateer was loaded and sent on his way. He no sooner cleared the runway, when we got a call "tanker 89 down wind. This meant that the 1st TBM was a few miles away and approaching the airport. Tanker pilots had a bad habit of buzzing the San Bernardino freeway at a low altitude of 50 to 75 feet. This practice would startle motorists on the freeway and usually within a half hour the California Highway Patrol (CHP) would show up at the airport looking for the offending pilot and aircraft. Lucky for the pilot that by the time the CHP got there, the aircraft had been reloaded and sent on his way. We always cooperated with the CHP. We would ask the officer to describe the aircraft. Usually we would be told that the aircraft was yellow. HMMM! All the TBMs were yellow. We would ask if anyone got the plane's number. The reply was always no. We would explain to the CHP officer that we had several aircraft that fit the general description but that based on his description, we could not tell which aircraft was the culprit. The Sunset fire was contained at days end and flight operations stopped. It should be noted that all fixed wing aircraft and helicopters working on fires are not allowed to fly ½ hour before sunset. Aircraft may not be dispatched to a fire ½ hour before sunrise. All fires on National Forest are named and assigned a number. Usually the name that is assigned comes from a distinct landmark near the point where the fire is first reported. We later found out that the Sunset fire had been started when a super sonic jet from Norton Air Force Base had lost control and had dived at full throttle into a slope a few hundred feet in front of Sunset lookout. Sandy the person who had been manning the lookout at the time recovered from the shock of seeing the accident and went on to complete the fire season.

Life at Chino airport could get quite dull. If there were no fires, there was not too much to do. We would do the routine jobs like keep the lead planes washed and waxed. We also made sure that our truck was also kept washed and waxed. When there was nothing else to do, we would look for something mischievous to do. One of our favorites was to play a prank on a pilot. Pilots often would pull a chaise lounge under the wing of their airplane and take an afternoon nap. On very slow days, we would sneak up on the sleeping pilot and fill his Wellington boots with gravel. After warning the rest of the personnel that a joke was in progress, we would go back to the tower and sound the fire siren. The pilot would jump up from his nap and start to run but with his boots full of gravel, he would usually fall down. It takes a lot of effort to get a Wellington boot filled with gravel off of ones foot. The gravel has to be removed one rock at a time.

One evening about 2:00 AM the phone woke me out of a sound sleep. Unfortunately the phone was on my wife's side of the bed. She did not move or answer the phone. I was forced to climb over her and answer the phone. The voice on the other end of the phone was Chuck Culver, who at the time was the lead dispatcher at Arcadia.

Chuck advised me that a fire had started in Millard Canyon and that we would need to have the airport operational by sunrise. I got dressed quickly and drove to the Arcadia Center where we kept our truck. In route to Arcadia I visualized Millard Canyon as that was one of the favorite places that I had gone hiking with the Boy Scouts. I remember wondering where the fire was in the canyon.

In 1960 Arcadia was the home of the dispatch center, the Forest Service Equipment Development Center and the Angeles Forest Engineers. It was located just off of double drive in Arcadia. By the mid 1980's the Equipment Development Center had moved and the Arcadia compound had become the headquarters for the Angeles Forest Supervisor.

I put gas in our truck the went to dispatch to wait for my boss and report in. Our dispatcher, Chuck Culver told me that he had ordered several Indian crews to assist with fire suppression activities. It was common in the 1960's for Indian tribes to provide fire fighters. We also used inmate labor from Los Angeles County and the California Division of Forestry (CDF).

My boss arrived and we departed for Chino airport which was about a 45 minute drive from Arcadia. It was really eerie at the airport driving through the 12 O' Clock high movie set in the dark. We passed the B 17 that was used by the movie studio and progressed out to our control tower. Sitting on the line were 3 TBMs and two PBY aircraft. Parked off to the side were our two lead planes, the B17 and several other fire fighting aircraft. We were the first to arrive but soon pilots, aircraft mechanics and ground support people began arriving.

Soon the sun started peeking over the horizon and the zone pilot, Ken Benish and lead plane pilot Sam Smith got into their T34 aircraft and started taxiing for take off. We got on the radio and gave them the coordinates of the fire. We also checked to see if any of the pilots had arrived at our airport on the desert side of the San Gabriel mountain range. This particular airport, Grey Butte, had been used during World War II as a place where glider aircraft were stored. The facility was equipped with an office trailer, a mobile telephone and 3 TBM aircraft. A couple of the pilots commuted to work using their own aircraft and the other pilot a support mechanic would drive to the site. This place was desolate with nothing around for many miles. The only method of contacting Grey Butte was to call the mobile phone operator and have her connect us to the mobile telephone at Grey Butte. We got through on the mobile phone and found out that there were a couple of pilots onboard and ready to go.

We gave the order to load the TBMs noting that one of the pilots Bill Drule had not yet arrived at the Chino airport. Soon the two TBMs that had pilots took off and headed north east towards the fire. These were followed by the two PBYs. A short time later, Bill Drule arrived. He explained that dispatch was very late in contacting him. Needless to say that we were happy to see Bill as he was rated as an initial attack pilot and was probably the best pilot stationed at Chino. Bill's plane had been loaded with borate and was ready to go. It only took him about 5 minutes to get into position and take off.

Bill was a World War II pilot who had flown TBM aircraft during the war. He had been quite lucky as 3 of his wartime planes had been shot out from under him. Bill had a young bride and a new baby. He also owned a Piper Tri Pacer and had offered to teach us how to fly and get our pilot's license. He told us that all we needed to do was pay for gas and oil to cover the cost of operating his plane. I was getting ready to take him up on his offer as I had always wanted to learn how to fly.

We got all the aircraft launched and working on the fire. If you have ever worked in a control tower that tracks and dispatches air tankers you know what the air net radio sounds like. It's like being in a war and having all your aircraft in a dog fight. By late morning, we got a call from dispatch telling us to hold our returning aircraft. The fire boss was going to use helicopters to work on some hot spots that the fixed wing aircraft could not drop on successfully. Needless to say, our pilots were not happy to be put on hold and being forced to wait for the helicopters to do their thing. The one good thing was that it was lunch time and the catering truck had just arrived.

The pilots gathered around the lunch truck gathering up soggy sandwiches soft drinks and candy bars. About the time that everyone had their lunch, dispatch called to request that we start the air tankers. The first one out was Bill in his newly rebuilt TBM Eight Zero. Just before he left he ran up to the tower and gave me his lunch. He ask me to save it for him. I put it in a safe place under the front counter, Eight Zero was the newest TBM in our fleet and had been in service about one or two weeks. Eight Zero was freshly painted. The colors were bright red and white, The number "80" was painted on the tail. Hopefully Bill would not buzz the freeway in this airplane as it could be easily identified.

We spaced the aircraft at five minute intervals and soon the radio came alive with the pilots talking to the lead planes. I remember hearing Sam Smith ask Bill Drule "why didn't you drop. Bills reply was that for some reason the load had not released. He told Sam that he was going to go around and get in line. Sam turned his attention to the next tanker that was in line for a drop.

Soon tankers began arriving back at Chino. The ground crews filled the retardant tanks and some of the aircraft were refueled. I began clearing the aircraft for takeoff at five minute intervals. Tanker 63 who was second in line for takeoff called me and requested an early departure. His reason was that Eight Zero had been the first aircraft out and for some reason had not returned to Chino. Tanker 63 told me that he was going to fly by the last known location of Eight Zero. He also requested that I check with the Van Nuys airport to see if Eight Zero had gone in there to refuel.

I called Van Nuys and was told that they had not seen our airplane. I checked the dispatch log and I could see that Eight Zero had been out a long time and was indeed overdue. Eight Zero did not respond to our calls over the air net. Twenty minutes later tanker 63 called me. He simply said Eight Zero had crashed. Tanker 63 gave us a location and we called Arcadia dispatch to see if we could get someone in to see if Bill had survived. In a matter of a few minutes the Los Angeles County Sheriff called to let us know that their helicopter was over the crash site and that there were no survivors. This was no surprise as it is very rare that a pilot survives a crash. I called Dispatch in Arcadia and requested that a team be sent in to retrieve the pilot. A team was dispatched. As all this was going on lead plane pilot Ken Benish returned to the airport and prepared to notify Bill's wife of the accident. Before Ken left on his unpleasant mission, the Los Angeles County Coroner called to tell us where the body would be taken. In this case Bill would be taken to the mortuary that was the closest to the accident. Ken left the airport to see Bill's wife.

Needless to say this all made quite an impression on me as I was just a young man who had never dreamed that I would be in the middle of an accident of this type. I hoped that this would never happen to me again. At the time, I felt like I had lost a good friend and I really worried about what would happen to Bill's wife and young son.

A few days later, Mr. Sullins (Sully), the owner of the B17 and an air charter service brought his DC 3 to Chino. He transported most of the pilots and friends of Bill's family to the funeral which was in Santa Barbara. I was left pretty much by myself at the airport in case we had any new fires.

The final report on Bill's death was that he had died of an apparent heart attack. The coroner told us that this was a common cause of death in a person who could see that he was about to die in a violent way. One question I think all of us had on this incident was: Would Bill still be alive if he had been flying his other tanker, TBM Eight Nine?

The summer progressed, and I finally got a few flying lessons. It all started on a flight in our T34 zero two ZULU. We were going over to Burbank airport to check on an aircraft that was being overhauled at Potter Aircraft. Shortly after we departed Chino our flying mechanic, Bob Clark, got on the radio and told me to look out across the wing of the aircraft. He told me to pay attention to the position of the wing as we were flying at about 5000 feet and the aircraft was level. He told me to take the stick and slowly move it from left to right. I did this. Bob then proceeded to walk me through several procedures including making turns, climbing and descending. Bob took over when we got close to the Burbank airport. He told me to follow through with him by holding onto the stick and lightly letting my feet touch the rudder pedals. One thing I will never forget about the Burbank airport is the high tension power lines that one had to fly over to land at Burbank. In later years I have looked for those power lines from commercial aircraft and have not been able to see them. It is possible that those particular power lines were moved. As time permitted, Bob showed me how to preflight the T34, start up the aircraft and taxi. I am sure that I would have learned a lot more but fire season ran out.

Our Chino unit had a C47 aircraft assigned to it. This aircraft was stationed at Chino and was to be used for smoke jumpers. The aircraft was on loan from Norton Air Force base. Frequently the zone pilot and Bob Clark would take this aircraft up to practice shooting landings. If I could get away, I would go with them. We would also exchange aircraft with the Air Force about once a month. Bob was especially interested in getting all the hours he could in this airplane as he was working on getting his multi engine rating. The C47 was the military version of the DC 3 which had been used a lot by the airlines in the early 1950's. In fact my first flight ever as a boy was on a United DC 3 which took us from Los Angeles to see my grandmother in Bakersfield. Two things I remember about riding in the Chino C47 were I tried to get into the airplane without a ladder, I realized how high off the ground the door to the aircraft was. I remember pulling myself up to get into the plane. Usually, I would take a crouched position between the two pilots and hang onto their seats as we made our touch and go landings. One time when we approached Norton to exchange aircraft, we got a warning from the tower that there was an un identified aircraft in the approach pattern. We finally figured out that the tower had not been monitoring our calls to them as we approached the base.

There was a lot of interest in the Forest Service concerning the length of the drop zone of the B17. To get this information, we filled the B17 tanks with water and then had the plane fly along the long runway at Chino and make a water drop. We then measured the distance covered by the water drop. The conclusion was that a B17 drop was about a mile in length. This was impressive as often the bombers would drop just in front of a progressing fire. Remember that the Borate and Bentonite that we were using would cling to the brush and the retardant was fireproof. What this all meant was that a B17 could create an effective fire break about 1 mile long.

Another experiment conducted by the Arcadia Equipment Development Center was to test wind machines. Every year the Forest Service gets a lot of suggestions on how to eliminate forest fires or put them out. One suggestion that I remember during my career was to install a sprinkler system forest wide. It sounds simple enough except that in Southern California there is not very much available water to support such a system. Then you need to consider the vegetation which in many cases is quite dense. You also need to consider the steep terrain. Put all this together and there is no way that you can build a Forest wide sprinkler system. Anyhow the Forest Service got a suggestion that a machine could be used to blow out a forest fire. There were a lot of skeptics, but the person who made the suggestion had a lot of political clout. The test took place at the airport and as it turns out, the wind machines that were used for the test already had a use namely the movie business.

The problems associated using this equipment were:

When you blow hard into an oncoming fire you create what is referred to as the clamshell effect. What happens is the fire kind of spreads out then wraps its self around the machine that is producing the wind. These wind machines were quite large and were made using Lycoming aircraft engines mounted on trailers so that they could be moved. The size of these machines it would be difficult if not impossible to position them in a good location to fight an on coming fire. Truck trails used in fire fighting are unpaved, narrow and are not graded very well. This would limit the use of the wind machines to use on major highways.

The machines were top heavy which meant that one would need to be very careful to keep the machines from toppling over when transporting them through the forest. On the positive side, the wind machines were equipped with spray booms and you could pump water or fire retardant through the spray booms onto an oncoming fire. The testing of the wind machines ended and I guess nothing further ever happened with them.

The 1960 fire season took its toll on the Angeles Nation Forest. One large fire was the Johnstone Peak fire. In a matter of a couple of days, this fire consumed most of the San Dimas Experimental Forest. Following the Fire, Congress would appropriate an emergency fund to rebuild this Forest. Little did I know it at the time but the Johnstone Peak fire would change my life forever.

Back at the airport we had a couple of accidents. Thank God nobody got hurt. One afternoon a single engine Cessna was shooting landings on the long runway (21) at Chino. We watched him for a period of time then he made a perfect landing with his gear up. He was not in communications with the tower so it was impossible to notify him that his gear was up. We notified the FAA that the airport was closed and helped make arrangements to get the plane removed.

A few weeks later, one of the B25 pilots took off using the long runway (21). He was flying a World War II BT. The BT was his company plane that was used for pilots to commute between Chino and Orange County airports. The plane got about 10 feet in the air and the engine quit. Down came the plane hitting the end of the runway. The pilot made a great effort to turn onto the taxi way before he ran out of runway. He missed, ran off the runway into a freshly plowed field. This tore the landing gear off the aircraft and the plane nosed over into the dirt. The pilot was fired as he had taken off using an empty fuel tank rather than the tank that had enough fuel to get him home.

As fall approached, one of the local community colleges offered a couple of Forestry classes. I signed up for the Introduction to Forestry. My future boss Lisle Green was the instructor and if nothing else, it gave me the opportunity to meet Lisle and get to know him. There were other interesting people in the class. One of them was a Forest Service patrolman who worked on the Arroyo Seco District. The patrolman had been badly burned. Apparently a year earlier, he had been working on a fire and the fire blew up. He went to duck behind a truck but the person in the truck drove off leaving him exposed to the flames. He was lucky to survive.

In the Spring I would take Forest Engineering which helped me in my job and provided me with a valuable handbook that I carried to work daily. I learned how to use the tools of the trade including an Abney level, a transit, chain tape, staff compass etc. Lisle taught the class along with one of his associates Tim Plumb.

Fall operations at the airport turned to aerial seeding projects using a Forest Service twin Beech aircraft. The aircraft was equipped with equipment that would allow the dispensing of seed. The aircraft would fly along the contour of mountain slopes and would drop seed onto the burned slopes. A couple of crewmen would keep the hopper inside the aircraft full of seed. In the early 1950's the favorite seed use was mustard. By the late 1950's the favorite seed was winter ryegrass. Winter rye would germinate fast and in the spring would generate a new crop of seed. I have heard estimates of upwards of 20 tons per acre of seed produced from a good crop of ryegrass.

I thought that it would be a great experience to be one of the crewmen who kept the hopper loaded with seed. Someone told me that I was crazy as the flights were generally rough and if you had the tendency you could get sea sick. My fate was that instead of getting to fly in the twin Beech, I was detailed to a seeding project on the San Dimas Experimental Forest. The schedule was that I would work with the seeding helicopters 3 or 4 times a week. The other Air Service Manager, Frank, would fill in with the helicopter project on the days that I worked the airport. I was not happy about this assignment. I didn't want to leave the excitement of the airport and the security of the job that I had mastered during my first fire season.

A couple of days before I started the helicopter seeding project, I was sent over to meet the project leader. I met him at a small heliport off the Glendora Mountain road. When I arrived at the heliport, there were two Bell G-2 helicopters parked there. I made the mistake of walking behind one of the helicopters. The project leader, Verdie White yelled at me and told me you never walk behind a helicopter. This was because of the danger of being hit by the tail rotor (stinger). What a way to make a first impression with the person I was going to work with for the next few weeks. Verdie and I worked out the schedule and I would report to him first thing in the morning at the Glendora office.

There are restrictions to aerial seeding, the most important one being that you may not seed when the wind is in excess of 10 miles per hour (MPH). The wind will carry the seed and if you want to hit your target you need to stay with in the 10 MPH limit. In the rugged terrain of the San Dimas Experimental Forest, very early mornings are when one has the opportunity to fly with the minimum amount of wind. Usually the wind will exceed the 10 MPH limit by 10 AM. Because of this, our work day started very early. The schedule was to meet in Glendora at 3:00AM. Arrive at the heliport by no later than 4:00 AM. Bring the stake side truck with the initial load of seed to the heliport. Check the weather including the wind speed and relative humidity. We did this using a portable anemometer and wet bulb / dry bulb thermometers. By 5:00 AM the helicopter crew was there. The mechanic serviced the two ships and got them ready to fly. An interesting thing to me was that there was only enough fuel loaded onto the helicopter to complete one seeding flight. This is because of the weight factor associated with the seed. The less fuel the more seed you could load. The heliports were nothing more than a dirt area that had been cleared so that the helicopter could land and take off. Usually, the heliport was located on a ledge so that the ship could take off and quickly gain airspeed by letting gravity pull the ship down as it gained forward momentum.

Since this was a re vegetation project for the Experimental Forest, there were over 20 small watersheds that would be seeded with different mixtures of seed. All in all we would be seeding about 30,000 acres. Prior to seeding an area, the project leader, Verdie White would take the Helicopter on a recon flight showing the pilot the boundaries of the area to be seeded. To help identify the area, several lunch sacks were filled with white lime. The process was to fly down a ridge and mark it by dropping the lime bags from the helicopter. This is a truly fun experience. You remove the door from the helicopter before takeoff and as you fly down the ridge, you lean out the door and drop the bag of lime. The lime makes a large spot on the ridge that is very visible from the air.

We were usually forced to shut down our air operations by 9:00 AM. After we shut down we would spend the rest of our workday mixing seed and getting ready for the next day's operations. Many of the watersheds that were seeded got different kinds of grass seed. This was done to evaluate how well different types of grass would germinate and adjust to the dry climate of Southern California. Rice hulls were used to make up the volume of very small seed like bluegrass. There were combinations of seed mixed to see how different mixtures would work. Grasses in the mix were both annual and perennial grasses. Mixing and bagging the seed was a major project. To assist us a Los Angeles County inmate crew was used. In the 1960's the Forest Service used a lot of inmate labor to get the job done. Both County and state inmate crews were utilized. These crews also played a major role in Southern California fire fighting. At that time, prisoners considered being on one of these crews a major perk. It was my understanding that the competition between prisoners to get on a fire crew was quite keen. As a very young man, working with these inmates was quite intimidating to me. A good friend of mine who had been in the Army reserve with me was a county fireman who supervised one the crews we used. He had convinced me that Forestry was a good deal and had been keeping me informed as to when the exams for the Los Angeles County fire department were being given.

One day when I was working at the airport, the dreaded phone call came. We had received enough rain to end the fire season and

Arcadia Dispatch gave the order to shut down the airport and layoff the seasonal crew. This was going to be my last day in the Forest Service until the spring when it would be time to open the airport and get ready for fire season. Needless to say I went home very depressed. Since my early teens I had always worked and I frankly did not know how I was going to handle unemployment. About eight o'clock that night, I got a phone call. It was from Verdie White. Verdie ask me if I would be interested in finishing the seeding project at the Experimental Forest. I told him yes and I was transferred to the Experiment Station the next day.

PART II:
FIRE RESEARCH

Working on the National Forest

Project Flambeau

An Education

A Changing Career

RESEARCH

For background the San Dimas Experimental Forest is located on the Angeles National Forest. Due to the nature of the research the area is closed to public entry. There is at least one unique area in the Forest which has been classified as a Research Natural Area. This area has a very old stand of Ponderosa Pine which generally does not grow in Southern California. How did these trees get there ? A small map of the experimental Forest is shown below.

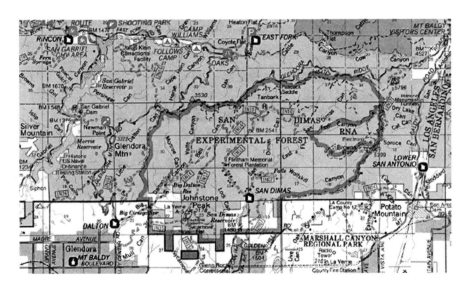

San Dimas Experimental Forest

As mentioned earlier, I was transferred to the San Dimas Experimental Forest temporarily to finish the helicopter seeding project that I had been assigned to. I would most likely be laid off when the seeding project was completed.

As the seeding project progressed, I seemed to be getting more and more responsibility. Because I had learned how to read topographic maps in the army and Boy Scouts, the project leader Verdie White had me take the helicopter out to recon the pilot and mark ridges for the next seeding area. This became one of my favorite parts of the job. There is nothing like bombing ridge tops with bags filled with lime. Occasionally the pilot would chase a deer with the helicopter. The poor animal seemed to panic at the sound of the big bird chasing it. The maps that I used to recon were copies of the original map and had been copied with a thermofax machine. In the very early 1960's Xerox technology either did not exist or was not in common use. The thermofax used a heat sensitive paper that was a light brown in color. After several days of being handled, a common problem was that the paper would just crumble up in ones hands. We always had to carry several copies of the map with us.

As fall progressed, the seeding project was winding down. I dreaded going to work as I was quite fearful that I would get my lay off notice. Finally, the flying/seeding part of the project ended and I was asked to do some simple analysis of what we had accomplished. What was needed was the total number of hours that we had flown, total number of acres and total lbs. of seed that had been put in each area. The seed totals needed to be reported by seed type. Examples were annual rye, perennial rye, blue grass, mustard, tall wheat, combinations of seed etc. This report took a few days as the only tools I had was a pad of paper and an adding machine.

A couple of days before the reports were completed, Verdie approached me and ask if I would be interested in working for the Fuel Break Project during the winter months. To me this was great news as I thought it would give me an opportunity to work through the winter and then return to the airport for the summer fire season. What nobody bothered to tell me was that when my 180 day appointment ran out, that I would have to be laid off for a period of time. Thinking that my job was secure for at least the next year, I told Verdie that I would be more than happy to work for the project.

The Fuel Break Project was originally assigned to Range Research. It would be transferred to Fire Research when the Forest Fire Laboratory in Riverside California opened in 1963. The idea behind Fuel Break was to convert ridge tops from chaparral which could be highly combustible to grass. Chaparral typically burns very hot while grass burn temperatures are relatively low. The Fuel Breaks would be 200 to 400 feet wide and would have a dirt road running down the middle of it so that men and equipment could get into an area quickly to make a stand against an approaching fire. It would also provide a relatively safe area for fire fighters to work from.

The concept sounds simple enough, all you need to do is clear off a large area of brush from a ridge top and plant it with grass. The Fuel Break in some cases could be used to graze sheep or cattle. Although the concept was simple, the doing it part was quite complex. In Southern California, the main cover type is mixed chaparral. Mixed chaparral, is comprised of Chamise, Toyon, Manzanita, Scrub Oak, Ceanothus, etc. Clearing the brush in its self is a major project unless the area of interest has recently burned. Clearing an unburned area takes hundreds of man hours per mile. Clearing a recently burned area is relatively easy and does not require near the effort.

Clearing the Fuel Break is the first step in the process. This was generally followed by seeding and hoping that we would get enough rain to establish a good crop of grass. The most difficult part of building Fuel Breaks is the rapid growth and return of the native chaparral. Within a few months of a fire in Southern California, the native plants begin to regenerate. As one walks through the burned area he can see sprouts appearing at the base of the native plants. If you look closely at the ground you can see many seedlings taking root. Getting rid of the native plants becomes a major problem. To accomplish this, the Fuel Break Project used different kinds of herbicides. In the early 1960's 24D and 245T were the most popular herbicides used by the project. These two chemicals had been in agricultural use since the early1940's. Most people don't realize it but if herbicides weren't widely used, the world would starve. One of the big problems that would confront the Fuel Break Project was that many of the native plants were very difficult to kill. One last thought on this subject is that many of the herbicides we used in Fuel Break are categorized as plant hormones. The theory is that the plant will grow its self to death in a very short period of time. If you have ever been in an area that has been treated with a herbicide, you will see the plant curling up and twisting into strange shapes. A common use of herbicides around the house is in lawn fertilizers. Weed and Feed would be a good example.

My first projects with Fuel Break were seeding projects. As a start we selected several small areas to seed and test how well the different kinds of seed would germinate and grow. We were also very interested to see if the grass would survive. We also would try several different kinds of seeding techniques. One of the first projects was to select a couple of small watersheds and employ a technique called waddling.

Waddling is where you take a special hoe and follow the contour of the watershed at 1 or 2 foot intervals and dig a shallow trench. In our case we would seed the trench with barley and a small amount of ammonium sulfate (16-20-0). The seed and fertilizer, would then be covered with about an inch of soil. Hard work? You bet. We worked with prison crews about 20 inmates per crew. We showed them where to plant and how to do it. The job was then to observe the planting crew to make sure that the job was done properly. After planting, the barley germinated in just a few weeks. Within about a three year period, the watersheds would become primarily barley watersheds.

My project shared resources and people with the Watershed Management Research Group. The common interest for the two groups was to modify the land cover type for fire control purposes and to see if there was any way to get the watersheds to yield more water. If successful maybe it would help with Southern California's water problems. One thing that research wanted to know was how much water was being used up by the grass cover. To help figure this out, we set up plots that were seeded with ryegrass. We then bored down about 20 feet using a bit/auger. When the hole was complete, we installed a brass pipe that would allow us to measure soil moisture using a neutron probe. The theory of the probe was that a small source of radio active radium beryllium would send out fast neutrons. When the neutrons came in contact with hydrogen, they would return slow neutrons to a recorder that we set up. The plot that I had was relatively small and I only had about 10 sites to read. I would place the probe in one of the brass pipes and lower it 1 foot at a time. It would take the recorder 3 or 4 minutes to take a reading. I was sure glad that I didn't carry the probe very far as it had a heavy lead shield that protected you from the radiation. I had a friend, Jim Clark who got the task of carrying the probe for several miles in two fairly large watersheds.

When using the probe, you would wear a dosimeter which would tell you how much radiation you had gotten during the days work. You also wore a film badge that was sent to the USDA Radiological safety officer every couple of weeks to make absolutely sure that you had not received a large dose of radiation.

Several weeks into this project, I returned to the office and read my dosimeter. The reading was off the scale and panic set in. Radiation can be fatal or have other serious lasting effects on a person. I quickly tracked down the local Radiological safety officer and ask him what I should do.

(Neutron Probe)

He calmed me down and told me to send my film badge in for processing. He also told me that the probe had a reputation. For all the guys who had used it, their wife's immediately got pregnant. This is contrary to science. One of the effects of radiation is that overexposure can render a human sterile. Up until that time, my wife had had one miscarriage. Since the miscarriage, my wife had not been able to get pregnant. At this point of our marriage, we were getting ready to see a specialist to find out why my wife couldn't get pregnant. The report from my film badge came back a couple of weeks later and the problem was most likely a failure of the dosimeter. A couple of months later, I got the good news, my wife was pregnant with our first child.

We contracted for a D-6 CAT to clear dead burned brush in several areas. As the land got cleared, we would either use a range land drill to seed or we would have an inmate crew plant what was believed to be fire resistant plants. We got the plants from the Forest Service Nursery located on the Arroyo Seco District. The plants were Salt Bush and 3 different varieties of Cistus. The Cistus is not native to the United States and had originally been imported from the Mediterranean. Later experiments in the lab would show that the Cistus was indeed fire resistant. You could take a butane torch and hold the flame directly on the plant. The leaves would melt instead of burn. The problem that we found was that when leaves and small branches died, the dead material became very flammable. The Salt Bush had a different kind of problem, rodents loved it and getting the plants to survive longer than a couple of weeks was a real chore. The research on flame resistant plants would later be turned over to Dr, Nord who would work on this project for several more years on developing fire resistant plants for the national forest.

On relatively flat land we used the rangeland drill to seed different kinds of grass seed. A rangeland drill looks like a disking tool that you pull behind a tractor. The difference is that there is a hopper mounted over the disk. The flow of seed can be controlled so you can seed an area heavy or light. You can also add fertilizer to the mix to help the seed germinate. We would ride on the back of the drill and make sure that all the seed got dispensed into the soil. On one occasion, I almost lost my left arm. I wore an army fatigue coat in the early mornings when it was quite cool. The hopper on the drill was equipped with small L shaped arms that would spin as the drill moved. One early morning as I was riding on the drill and sweeping the seed into the drills down spout, one of the L arms grabbed my coat and my arm was slowly getting wrapped into the workings of the machine. Lucky for me that the Cat Operator was alert and heard me yelling for him to stop.

(Range Land Drill)

As we were busy seeding different areas on the Forest, the Watershed Management group was doing major construction at the mouth of the small watersheds. Forest Service Engineers were busy building cement weirs. The weirs had precise measurements and were constructed so that runoff during rain storms could be measured by humans and instrumentation that would be installed in the weir. In the Forest Service you always think of fire fighting. In 1961 and into succeeding years, Foresters and Technicians who worked on the Experimental Forest would be called for Storm Duty. Other than standing in the rain and getting wet, there were a couple of real adventures to come when I was called for storm duty.

Grass, brush and all kinds of weedy plants started to grow on the forest following the first rain storm. The Project Leader Lisle Green, began working with one of the experiment station biometricians to setup a scheme for sampling the results of our seeding projects and getting the information into a computer for analysis. When the sampling design had been accomplished, Lisle called me into his office and let me know that I would be heading up sampling crews and that we would need to establish permanent sampling plots in 20 plus watersheds. Each watershed would have at least 36 sampling sites and would be sampled 3 times a year. So that the plots could be relocated during the sampling cycle, a precise description of the location of the plot had to be written. Once located, the plot would be marked with a wooden stake. Setting this up was not easy. We had to carry wooden stakes with us and use Forest Survey equipment to get the job done. Since there was a lot of hiking needed to reach a sampling site, we would do the initial sampling when we established the sampling plot. The sampling process was to sample four square feet per plot and to identify all the plant and items in the plot including grass, brush, herbaceous material, rock and litter. This meant that I had a lot of learning to do as I didn't know very much about the different kinds of plants that covered the area. There were a couple of books available that would assist us with this effort. If we got stuck, I would take a sample back to Lisle and he would make the identification. As the sampling progressed, new plants were listed and coded so that the data could be entered into the computer. As the sampling project progressed, I would head up a crew of about ten technicians, training them in how to identify and record the different kinds of plants. On an average workday, we would cover at least 10 miles on foot. To expedite the process, we would spot our trucks at the bottom of the canyon in the morning. We would then drive a truck to the top of the project where we would begin the days journey. Working on the slopes of the experimental Forest was difficult as the terrain was composed of decomposed granite. Because of the steep slopes and all that loose rock, I would wear out a pair of boots in about two months. You might think that the heals and soles of the boots would wear out but the first thing to go was the sides of the boots. The loose rock would literally cut the sides of the boots off.

The first year, sampling went pretty smoothly. By the second year, a few hazards got in our way. Poison Oak became a problem for some of the crew members. To build up an immunity, there were pills you could buy that would help you build up a tolerance for poison oak. Every sampling season, I would buy a bottle of Aqua Ivey which is a poison oak extract. You start by taking one pill a day and increase the dosage every week until the pills are gone. The pills helped me a lot. But some of my crew members were very allergic to poison oak and had to be taken off the project. For me, it was typical to spend the sampling season with a very mild rash on my legs.

A bigger danger was with all that grass seed the rodents had returned to the experimental forest. Along with the rodents came the rattlesnakes. We called the rattlesnakes buzz tails. In all the time that I spent on the experimental forest, I never got used to coming upon a rattle snake. In fact, one cool morning as I was tying flagging on a survey stake, I looked down and saw that familiar black and yellow pattern. You guessed it, I was standing right on top of a rattle snake. This created a dilemma. What do you do? The snake was pretty well pinned down but if I moved, it could strike. I thought about it for a couple of minutes and finally decided to jump off the snake. I think I broke the worlds broad jump record that day. When you hear about rattle snakes, you hear that they always rattle and give you a warning. This is not true. The snake that I stepped on never made a noise. We decided that we needed some kind protection. We wound up buying snake shapes which we wore religiously every day when we were sampling.

I will never forget this one crewman that I had who was always running through the grass and weeds. I kept telling him that one day he would be sorry as he would run into a snake. One day as I climbed to the top of a ridge, I saw this crewman with his snake stick, beating the grass in front of him and moving very slowly down the ridge. This is a common reaction after meeting a snake. The rest of us all got a good laugh out of this one.

The absolute worst area for finding snakes were the areas where we had planted barley. There were a lot of rodents in the barley and hence a lot of snakes. One day my partner and I started into one of these barley watersheds and a snake that was apparently quite near began to rattle. Soon another snake started to rattle, then another snake then another. What to do, you couldn't see any of them. We did the only thing we could think of we turned and ran out of the watershed.

The spring rolled around and in early May I was notified that my appointment was about to run out. I thought I could get a new appointment. Wrong! If nothing was done, I would have to be laid off for about 90 days. This was bad news indeed as the fire season would be well underway and the chances of me getting hired in the middle of the season were little to none. My boss Lisle Green, was not happy at the prospect of loosing me. He started working with our personnel office in Berkeley and found out that I could get a taper appointment because there were no established rosters for research technicians. Wow, I thought I had it made but there was one more obstacle. Walt Hopkins who was a program manager in Berkeley was worried that the new position in Fuel Break might not get funded beginning with the new fiscal year that would start the first of July. I don't know to this day how Lisle did it but he convinced Walt to step aside and let me get my appointment. I had to agree however, to remain in research and not return to the airport.

I celebrated getting a permanent appointment but I had to take a 25% pay cut which was tough. The other reductions in take home pay were medical insurance which we needed and withholding for retirement which in the early 1960s was much more than social security had been. When you are a federal employee, you pay into the government retirement system instead of social security. In 1960, social security was a 3% tax. Withholding for the government retirement program was 7%. All this resulted in my take home pay being about $110.00 every two weeks. My monthly house payment was about that much so the other $110.00 had to last the rest of the month.

Vegetation sampling continued into June. I heard that our project was going to do some helicopter spraying and I thought that this would give me a break from sampling. I was wrong. A different crew was brought in to do the helicopter work and me and my crew continued sampling. As the spraying project progressed, we started noticing its effects on the vegetation. The herbaceous plants began swelling up and taking on a twisted appearance. The chaparral plants had a similar effect. Within a few weeks, the herbaceous material was dead. Some of the brush also appeared dead. I would find out that some of the brush species like Chamise would actually die. The scrub oak would have a small setback and soon would resprout.

One Friday evening, I was asked if I would like to earn some overtime and work on the spraying project. I was very happy to do so. Helicopter spraying has much stricter restrictions. Wind speed can be no more than 5 miles per hour. This is because, the spray can be carried for miles by the wind and can affect foliage many miles away. We could not risk the herbicides being carried into the grape vineyards below the National Forest.

We had two productive weekend days of spraying. The winds cooperated and we were able to put in 8 hour days. Sunday, however would turn out to be a very bad day for me. We completed spraying and I returned home. As I was driving home, I remember thinking that we would have a little extra money which would help with our financial pinch. When I got home, I remember walking into the kitchen. My wife who was on the back porch saw me come in. She gave me a funny look and came into the kitchen. She told me that my dad had just died. This was a shock as my parents had been on a cruise which was going to Canada. The ship they were on was a German vessel that carried cars from Germany to the US. There were very few passengers on this boat and no doctor on board. My dad had died from a heart attack.

I had had a very high admiration for my father as he had made some real accomplishments during his life time. He had told me when I was a senior in high school that he had never graduated from high school. Somehow he had gone on and got accepted into law school. He had had to work at Western Auto to support himself while he attended college. Later in life, my dad had tried some famous cases when he was the United States Attorney. He had advanced in his career to become a federal judge. As a judge, he was very well known in the Los Angeles community. In fact my boss, Lisle Green, asked me if I was related to Judge Tolin. My dad and I had very different interests. As a young man, I was going to be a mechanic and own a gas station. I was always getting in trouble for modifying the family car. My dad was a work o holic and always brought work home. My dad's passing was quite a shock even though he had been in very bad health for a number of years. Following his funeral I went back to work.

For the next few months, I would experience a very strong presence. My dad was there with me as I worked out on the national forest. There were times that I could almost see him. Since that time, I have always felt that my dad has been there to guide me when I needed help. I mentioned this phenomenon to my mother and she had had a similar experience. She told me that the night when my dad passed away, she had gotten a very strong feeling that my grandmother Tolin was there with her and my dad as he passed away. This was a little strange as my mother and my grandmother in life had never gotten along.

During the summer, we continued sampling. The crew that had been helping went back to their assigned fire stations. I sometimes worked alone and at other times worked with another technician who would leave in the fall for a new assignment. Being in research, our primary assignment was research, however, we were subject to fire duty. During the first summer with the experiment station, we would always volunteer for fire duty but our generous offer was always ignored. This was because the fire season in 1961 was relatively slow. Things picked up in the 1962 fire season. There was a case where an arsonist devised a time delay device that would start a fire an hour or two after he had left the area. This particular device was driving the regional investigator nuts. Catching an arsonist is difficult as you almost have to catch him in the act. Elgin, who was the investigator devised a plan as this particular arsonist was setting fires about every two weeks. Some of the tactics that Elgin devised are still in use today by the Forest Service. Elgin had an office next to mine so I got to know him pretty well. It was interesting as Elgin had known my dad. Apparently my dad and Elgin had worked on several fire cases together with Elgin being the investigator and my dad being the prosecuting attorney. Elgin would soon be retiring and I thought that being a regional investigator would be a neat job to get. I set this as a goal but my hopes were short lived as the District Fire Control Officer, Bill Longacre stepped in and took the job when Elgin retired. A special note, in the early 1960s the California region had two law enforcement investigators. By the mid 1980s, each National Forest would have at least one full time law enforcement person and in most cases the Forest would have several investigators. Many of these investigators were part time.

After several weeks, Elgin had pretty much figured out who the arsonist was. The person was a barber who worked in a small barbershop in Claremont, California. The Forest Service put this person under 24 hour surveillance. Sure enough, a few days later, they caught the person setting his device out in the National Forest. Just a quick note about arsonist. The majority of these people are mentally ill and need medical treatment. Most of the other arsonists are people who have a grudge and are trying to get back at someone or something.

Following the arrest of the arsonist, a television drama was produced and shown on the Television series General Electric True. The series also did a show which focused on the life of Forest Service Patrolmen. Chuck Hartly was the patrolman that the series selected to highlight. The two television shows got the attention of the networks and about 18 months later, a TV series about the Forest Service came on the air. The Forest Service provided a technical advisor to the producer of the show. We were all pleased that television had taken note of the Forest Service. We were however very disappointed that the show was named Lassie and featured a dog as one of the stars. There are so many adventures in the Forest Service that could be filmed that it is really too bad that the show had to focus on a dog.

In the fall of 1961, the small watersheds that had been set up with weirs and instrumentation were ready for manning when rain storms passed through the Southern California area. Each weir was equipped with a flow recorder. During rain storms, two man crews would be sent out to man about 5 weirs in 5 different watersheds. Duties included making sure that the flow meters started and continued to run. The crew was also equipped with jump sticks that would allow them to record the depth of the water flowing though the weir. The crew would also take periodic grab samples of the water moving through the weir. The grab samples would later be analyzed in the lab to see how much mud and debris had passed through the weir at different times during the storm.

Other than the inconvenience of being wet and cold during a storm, the storm duty job sounded like it would be a relatively safe one. Wrong! I remember being in a small watershed and having my partner say what is that noise? We found out rather quickly. The sound was rocks and debris being pushed very quickly down the watershed. When you could see this coming, it was almost too late to get out of the way. If a person was caught in this flood of rock, water and debris, he would most likely not survive. Our escape path was to quickly climb the side of the canyon wall and hope that we could get high enough before the water level got too high.

There was a case where one research forester and his assistant tried to outrun one of these floods in their International Harvester 4X4 truck. The truck could not move fast enough and they literally had to abandon it and climb the canyon walls for safety. The truck on the other hand just disappeared. It was completely covered with mud and rocks. The road crew found the truck the following spring when they were rebuilding the road through the bottom of the canyon.

During major storms we would spend our off hours at Tanbark Flat. Tanbark had originated during the war. It was equipped with several residences including an Administrators residence, a two storey house, a three bedroom house and a barracks. There were also warehouses and a barn which housed equipment and supplies. The residences were well furnished and had multiple fireplaces in many of the rooms. Firewood was not a problem as many of the plantations surrounding Tanbark had been destroyed by the fire. The trees that survived the fire were later killed by bark beetles. One of the perks of working for the Forest Service was that you could rent one of the residences for about $25.00 to $35.00 per month. Rent included utilities. I had considered moving to Tanbark at one time but access was 20 miles of narrow dirt road which would take you to the nearest town of Glendora. The other thing was that I had purchased a house before joining the Forest Service so it didn't make much sense to move.

When you would leave home for storm duty, often you could be gone for a couple of weeks. Since there were no telephones at Tanbark, your family usually would not hear from you while you were gone.

In the spring of 1962, my partner and I were sent off to fire school in preparation for the upcoming fire season. We were trained to be Crew Bosses. In today's world the terminology used by the Forest Service in California, has changed significantly from the early 1960's. Unlike other parts of the United States all fire fighting agencies have adopted the same terminology for firefighting and natural disasters. Some examples are: Radio protocol has moved from using the ten code to plane text. Instead of saying 10-4 (ok), you would respond by saying "copy". Radio frequencies in California are now managed so that fire agencies can talk to one another during an emergency. In the late 1970's, an Incident Command Center was built and equipped in Southern California. The site is normally not manned unless there is some kind of a major emergency taking place. In the 1980's, this center would be jointly manned by different high ranking officials from different state and federal agencies.

Following the training, I would get dispatched to fires. Usually, I did not get assigned to a suppression team. This is because most of the Fire suppression teams were treated as complete units such as a tanker crew would have its full complement of personnel when dispatched to a fire. A Hot Shot crew would also have its full compliment of personnel. Many of the very difficult jobs that require a lot of physical labor was done by inmates from county and state prisons. When dispatched to a fire, I would usually get assigned to a Fire Behavior Team. Our job was to look at issues related to fire weather, fuel and terrain as well as other factors that might affect the overall strategy for fighting the fire. I also worked on the heliports managing the sites as well as getting passengers who were being shuttled to the front lines safely on and off the helicopters.

I remember one night when I was working with a fire behavior team being stationed on a ridge top directly across the canyon from where the major action was taking place. It was about 2 in the morning and I got this frantic call. I was advised that there had been a significant change in the wind direction and that the fire had changed course and was heading directly toward a large group of firemen who were working in the canyon. The fire was approaching from below the crews which was really bad news because a fire can and does burn very hot when making a very fast run up hill. The person who called me on the radio told me that they had been trying to reach the crews by radio but because of their location, the crews apparently could not be reached. I was asked to try and notify the crews to evacuate the canyon ASAP. Gulp! What if I couldn't get through? I quickly turned my attention to the radios I had brought with me. I began calling the crews that were located in the canyon across from me. A big relief, as soon as I gave the first call, I got a response. Soon, I observed a very large caravan of fire trucks leaving the area in danger. Thank God, nobody got hurt that night.

Fire camps in the 1960's were quite a complex organization. In many ways, a fire camp was set up very similar to a military operation. As crews and equipment arrived at the fire camp, they would check in with the timekeepers who would designate an area to go and wait for an assignment. Crews and equipment could get an immediate assignment to work on the fire. There was a plans and logistics section, first aid section, a tool crib where you could go and get the equipment that you needed for a fire assignment. Many of the older more experienced firemen would make sure that they got new shovels, axes, snakebite kits etc. Since this was a fire, most of the equipment that was issued from the fire cache would not be returned. Many crews would look forward to a fire to replenish their units supplies. Very large areas were set up to feed the firefighters. The cooking was done mostly by inmates who were experienced with cooking large volumes of food. If you were hungry, you could go to the mess area anytime and get a great meal. It was not uncommon to be able to get a nice thick steak. The American Red Cross was always in the major fire camps. They would make sure that the fire fighters got the little luxuries in life that they needed. Items like cigarettes, candy etc were always available at fire camp. If you went through a pair of boots you could go to the commissary and order a new pair of boots which would be delivered in a relatively short period of time. A special note, when I worked in freshly burned areas of the San Gabriel Mountains, I would wear out a pair of boots in about two months. The boot soles would be ok but the rocks and loose gravel would literally cut through the sides of my boots in a short period of time. Personal items like boots would be deducted from your pay check. During major fires, the Forest Service would often contract with local restaurants to prepare box lunches for the fire crews that were working on the fire lines. One of the hazards of these lunches was that there was no refrigeration and lunches would sometimes spoil making the crewmen sick. If you were working on a fire line you were often warned that if your lunch came with any kind of mayonnaise on the sandwich, don't eat it. You would think that the people working with the restaurants would warn the sandwich makers to be careful. But I guess that would be too much to ask.

It was a common practice for all firefighters to stay in the fire camp when off duty. It didn't matter which fire agency you were with, it could be federal, state or county. If you didn't bring your own sleeping bag with you, you would be issued a paper sleeping bag. These paper sleeping bags did a fairly good job all things considered. By the mid 1980's, the California State crews would begin staying in motels and eating in restaurants when they were off duty. This would make the CDF crews one of the most expensive crews in the fire fighting business. I remember one late afternoon working a fire near Santa Barbara. I had just returned to fire camp and was getting ready to settle down for the night. The fire made a run and the next thing we knew was we were battling the fire right there in fire camp. A few hours later and a lot of hard work we were able to save the fire camp.

One hot summer afternoon, I was working on a fire near Idyllwild. Since it was hot I had my shirt sleeves rolled up. This was against the rules when working on a fire but it was hot and at the time I was no where near the fire. Four of us got invited to start backfiring an area that was ahead of the advancing fire. The hope was that we could as a minimum slow the advancing fire down and if we were lucky, we might even be able to stop the advance of the fire in that sector. I went to my designated area and began setting the backfire using a drip torch. Within a very short period of time I had a good fire started. Pretty soon the fire began to explode and flames were reaching towards the sky. I finished the line that I was firing and began moving towards the fire break that was just a few yards away. I don't know if the fire was taking my oxygen or if I was just tired and out of shape but I was finding it very hard to move out of the way of the fire and get to the safety of the fire break. I finally made it and as I walked away from the fire, I could feel the skin on my arms cooking and blistering from the heat. I now understood why you never work a fire with your sleeves rolled up. The other thing that I learned was that fires move very quickly and you need to be able to access a safe area quickly if necessary. Up until that time, I had always thought that a firefighter in good shape could get away from an advancing fire. I learned how wrong I was that hot afternoon.

During the summer of 1963, the Forest Fire Laboratory in Riverside California opened. I went through the normal frustrations of being transferred. I sold my house in San Gabriel and put money down on a new comparable home in Riverside, California. When I went for my interview with the mortgage company I was turned down because I only made $5000.00 per year. I was purchasing a $21,000.00 home and was putting $11,000.00 down. My realtor was very angry. His comment was that nobody puts that much money down and gets turned down for a loan. I finally got a loan and we were able to move in. Part of the summer of 1963 was dedicated to working on getting our part of the new lab set up. We then went back to our normal routine of doing vegetation sampling. This required us to drive back to the San Dimas Experimental Forest.

One of the new positions that was filled at the Fire Lab was a photographer. I thought that this would be a great opportunity for advancement. My lobbying for the position didn't work and another person got hired.

By 1964, the Department of Defense contracted with the Fire Lab to study fire storms. The storms were supposed to represent the same kind of fire storm that would be created with the detonation of a nuclear device. The idea behind the study was to determine what would happen to homes in a typical subdivision if a nuclear device went off. To accomplish this, several test areas were setup in the Nevada desert. The project was scheduled to take about 3 years and would have several test fires. After about 1 year of site preparation, the Department of Defense failed to fund the project. This was a major financial problem for the Fire Laboratory. Up until that time, I had always assumed that if you had a permanent appointment with the government, your job would be relatively safe. How wrong I was. One Monday morning, we were directed to attend a mandatory meeting of all personnel. At the meeting, we were advised that because of the funding cuts, many personnel would be laid off and much of our equipment would have to be turned in. About 1/3 of the staff was laid off including the photographer so I guess I was lucky that I hadn't gotten that job. One year later the Department of Defense again funded the project. The project was code named FLAMBEAU. Project FLAMBEAU became an international effort with countries from all over the world participating.

The first project site that I was assigned to was located close to Mono Lake. The test site was about 50 acres. Piles of Pinon Pine were stacked into piles which were supposed to have the rough equivalent of a 3 to 4 bedroom house in each pile. The piles of pine were separated by dirt streets which were about the width of a subdivision two lane road. We worked 10 hour days and our off time was spent in a small Nevada community called Hawthorn. Hawthorn had 1 main casino and a couple of motels and that was about it. If you didn't gamble there wasn't too much to do at night other than watch the floor show at the main casino, the El Capitan. The Casino offered a gamblers special flight from Los Angeles to Hawthorne for $10.00. Forest Service and other personnel could get to the and from the test site quickly and cheaply.

I spent a couple of months working on this project and got my first experience handling explosives. In order to get the effect of a nuclear fire storm, we had to get everything to ignite at the same time. This was accomplished by wiring each pile of pine up with 6 blivits. The blivits were constructed of a soft plastic skin and were filled with napalm and black powder. At the top of the blivit, there was a blasting cap that would set off the charge. Each blivit had to be wired into the main line that would send an electrical charge through the site and would ignite the piles of pine all at the same time. I was quite disappointed because I was called back to the Fire Lab a few days before the fire was set off. I remember hearing that it was a big success and that we would proceed with the next burn which would be the largest of all the burns.

The following summer, I spent a lot of time working on the large site that was targeted for a fall burn. This site was impressive as not only were there piles of pine but we built structures on very large weighing platforms (load cells) It was the intent to weigh the platforms every few seconds to determine how quickly the fire was consuming the structure. The structures represented a typical home like the ones that were being built in the 1960's. To get the job done, I was given a crew of pickup laborers who spent most of their time working in mines in the central Sierra. My partners big John Moore, Dick Johnson and I rented an apartment in Bishop California as we would work on this project most of the summer. The commute from Bishop to the site was about 1 ½ hours each way. The site was located near Basalt Nevada. We would work 7 days a week 12 hours a day. In addition to building the structures on the weighing platforms, we also built instruments which had to be mounted on towers that overlooked the test site. You could not be afraid of height as many of the towers were 100' high and you had to climb the tower and wire the instruments in.

As fall approached, the test sight became very busy with people from all over the world working on their own special projects. Some areas within the test plots were closed to entry unless you had the proper security clearance. The day of the burn was just a couple of days away and we got briefed on what to expect and were assigned to a station where we would monitor the fire and its progress. The team to which I was assigned to was comprised of myself, my partner Dick Johnson and a crew of Navy combat photographers who had just arrived back in the United States. These guys had been taking combat photos in Viet Nam. All the instruments in the towers and on the weighing platforms were double checked to make sure that they were working properly. All equipment was hooked up to the recording equipment that would create tapes that would later be read into an IBM 7040 computer for analysis. A B-52 bomber was assigned to the project to measure heat radiation from the air. The flight of the B-52 would begin from an Air Force base near Salt Lake City, Utah. Our last major effort was to wrap as many instrument towers as we could with asbestos to keep the towers from melting during the fire. A few towers did not get this treatment and they melted about half way into the burn.

The morning of the burn started about 3:30AM. We drove from Bishop to the test site and reported in. We then went to our assigned area and met the combat photographers that we would be working with. In addition to the combat photographers, several fire suppression crews from the California Division of Forestry were assigned to our area.

Hopefully we would not need them. We also double checked to make sure that if necessary, we could evacuate the area quickly.

When the sun peeked over a ridge top it was about 7:00 AM. Radios kept in constant communications. The burn command post notified the FAA and the military that a major burn was about to take place and that the area was closed to all air traffic except our helicopters and our B-52. At 7:45 AM the final radio checks and testing of the instruments began and at 7:59 the final countdown. At 8:00 AM sharp the radio count began with 9, 8, 7, 6, 5, 4, 3, 2, 1, fire. There was a rumble that came with the explosion of the black powder. The site lit up with fire everywhere. We were stationed about 100 yards from the flames and you could begin to feel the radiation from the fire on your face and hands. The rest of our bodies were well protected with turnout coats and long pants. In the first minute of the fire the site came alive with all piles and structures burning. After two minutes the flames reached to the sky possibly going 100 to 200 feet into the air. A column of smoke went straight up then mushroomed out and iced over. This looked like the real thing.

About every 3 minutes, the B-52 would make a low level pass over the test site. One of the passes came after only about a minute, we kind of wondered about this and about a minute later, the B-52 that had just flown over us had turned around and was coming back. As we looked up, we could see a second B-52 coming straight at us. Everyone held their breath. Were we about to see a mid air collision of two B 52 bombers? It was a very close call but the two planes managed to miss each other. It turns out that from the air you would see a mushroom shaped cloud that was iced over. The cloud looked like a real "A" bomb had just gone off. From the air as you looked down on the test site, you could see what looked like a small city totally engulfed in flames.

It was this sight that had drawn the 2nd B 52 to fly over us and then turn around and return for a second look.

The main part of the burn took about an hour. The site following the burn was mostly ashes, a few piles that did not get fully consumed by the fire and several towers that had not been well enough insulated that were twisted and bent over making strange shapes on the desert floor. The towers that had been properly insulated stood straight and tall.

The day of the burn, there were all kinds of reports that came in from the surrounding communities about what people believed had been a nuclear explosion. Following the fire we got a chance to view the aerial photos both movies and still pictures of the fires. This was impressive. We remained at the burn area until the next day and then went into ground zero to take soil samples. Most people don't realize it but soil when exposed to very high temperatures becomes very water resistant. Our soil samples would be taken back to the fire lab for analysis. In later studies, scientist from UCLA would experiment with wetting agents to see if the water resistant factor could be broken down. If successful, maybe the flooding following a fire could be reduced.

Following the fire we returned to the fire lab and got back into the routine of vegetation sampling. We also got involved in doing vegetation fuel moisture testing along with fuel volume studies.

(Ernie Tolin Taking Soil Samples Project FLAMBEAU Top)
(Below my primary crew me, Big John Moore Dick Johnson)

My boss was beginning to show signs of frustration as he had spent a lot of time with the Station Biometrician and a computer person. The intent was that our vegetation surveys following the Johnstone peak fire would be analyzed and that my boss could publish the results of our vegetation surveys. In Forestry research, a researcher must publish his findings every year. If he is not able to publish, he will not get promoted and he may in fact be terminated. To help, I began trying to analyze a small portion of the data that we had collected. This was quite time consuming and my available tools were an adding machine and a rotary Monroe calculator. The calculator could multiply and divide which was quite useful but manually manipulating the reams of data was very time consuming. After three years of collecting data, we finally got some reports back from our Berkley office. The reports made absolutely no sense and there was no way that we could verify the data that had been provided back to us. In self defense, I began taking classes in computer programming at Riverside Community college. I lied to get into the first class as I did not want to take the time to go through the introduction class. This proved be a major mistake on my part but I managed to stay with it and get a B+ for my efforts. What I hadn't realized when I enrolled in the first programming course was that the course focused on programming in "Assembly" language. Assembly language programming is somewhat difficult and I spent most waking hours just trying to get my homework assignments done.

My boss was thrilled that I was learning programming and he made me promise to show him my report card. It was this promise that helped me stick with it and get a decent passing grade. Following my first programming class, I was able to convince my boss to send me to IBM school to learn how to program in Fortran. The class was a Fortran VI class and I spent a week in Los Angeles at the IBM education center. This was very frustrating for me as Fortran was nothing like the Assembly language that I had learned. I had a very difficult time trying to figure out how to write a simple program in Fortran. I returned to the fire lab and in my off hours worked at writing computer programs to accomplish simple tasks. Suddenly the light bulb went on and I discovered that programming was not all that difficult. I enrolled in the fall Fortran course at Riverside Community college where I learned different techniques for programming. During the next few years, I would take numerous courses in computer technology. At one point, I even thought that I would get a degree in computer science but this just didn't work out. The reason was that at this point in my life, I had a lot of college units but the colleges would not accept all the units. It went something like this. You could use most of your units that you had earned at another college and take 17 units at the local college then graduate. Or you could take many classes at the local college and use 17 units from other institutions. This didn't work for me as I had college units from UCLA, and three other institutions. I finally gave up and focused all my efforts towards learning as much about computer systems as I could.

I began writing simple computer programs to analyze the vegetation data that we had collected. I found out quickly that I could generate a lot of reports showing lots of trends from our seeding projects. I also began writing programs that analyzed the results of our fuel volume studies and our fuel moisture studies. Programming consumed about ½ of my work time and the other half I continued working as a technician.

One spring, I was called on to manage a helicopter spraying operation which included mixing herbicides managing the loading crew and re-conning the helicopter. Early one morning, the heliport got a call from one of our observers, Chuck Culver. Chuck reported that the helicopter had gone down into a canyon and had not come out. As the copter had been out of sight for several minutes, we began rescue operations. A rescue crew was sent in from the bottom of the canyon. Pat Hartless and myself started down a major ridge top. About ¾ of the way down, I spotted what looked like red flagging hanging on an old snag. It turned out that this was part of the copters tail rotor. We continued down the ridge until we found the helicopter which was located face down at the bottom of a water fall. The pilot was out of the ship and was trying to disconnect the battery. This is standard procedure in an accident of this kind. If you can disconnect the battery, you eliminate the possibility of an electrical fire. The team from the bottom of the canyon arrived and we carried the pilot out past the dam at the bottom of Bell Canyon.

(Helicopter Crash)

The herbicide that the copter had been carrying was in the small lake behind the dam and looked like a giant large white mushroom under water. The pilot was taken to the local hospital and was released a few hours later.

An investigation was started to look into the cause of the crash. The pilot had stated that the ship's bubble had burst and the ship started shaking then rolled over and crashed. The ultimate cause of the crash was that the helicopter had encountered some downed telephone lines that were draped across the canyon. The telephone lines had been out of commission for several years since the Johnstone Peak fire. The Forest Service would ultimately get sued for the loss of the helicopter by its insurance company. The Insurer would claim that the Government had been negligent in not warning the pilot of the downed phone lines which the insurer claimed was a hazard to navigation. A survey that the Forest Service did of the canyon showed that at the time the helicopter hit the phone lines, there was less than 12 inches of clearance for the rotor in the area where the crash occurred. I wound up having to testify in the case which was quite un nerving as the insurer was trying to make me the culprit by showing pictures of me taken earlier at the spot where the accident had occurred. In the photo, I was looking over the canyon and the downed phone lines. Since I was the guy who had re-conned the helicopter it had to be my fault. The Forest Service wound up paying for the lost helicopter. Because of the good investigation and the survey done in the canyon, the Forest Service concluded that there had been some kind of mechanical failure that caused the helicopter to go down. A final note, several years later, I realized that the first spots where we had seen the wreckage of the helicopter was several hundred feet up canyon from where the ship actually hit the wires. Since there were no wires near where the ship had crashed, I can only conclude that something had happened prior to the helicopter hitting the wires. It should also be noted that for this particular pilot, he had crashed 3 other helicopters that same year.

As time passed, I spent more and more time writing computer programs. After about a year, we got a questionnaire about the computer applications that we were using in the project. I took the questionnaire seriously and did a complete job writing a detailed description of what the applications did plus I drew simple flow charts showing what the programs actually did. My boss immediately got comments back from headquarters praising the job I had done. Ultimately, I would be assigned to manage the Riverside data processing section part time.

One of the challenges that I got when I took over the data processing sections was our headquarters had made a decision that the Fire Lab should have a high speed remote batch terminal. This was acquired through our cooperators at the UCLA campus computing network (CCN). I got our site ready for the terminal which included getting the proper electrical connections in place, air conditioning and most important data communications lines. In the early to mid1960's, high speed data communications was 2000 bits per second (BPS) to about 4800 BPS. The technology of that era used data compression to help speed up the data communications process.

The big day finally arrived and our terminal was delivered and IBM began the installation. It took the Customer Engineer (CE) about 2 weeks to determine that the terminal that we had received had a special feature that would not work with the computer at UCLA. The terminal was returned to IBM and we waited for about 90 days for the replacement terminal to be delivered. When it got there we discovered that it had the same special feature and we could not use the equipment. IBM put us on the top of the waiting list and the new terminal arrived in a couple of weeks.

Installation of the new terminal went pretty fast and after a couple of days we were ready to start testing the terminal to see if we could actually communicate with UCLA and run our programs at their facility. Since nobody at the local IBM office had ever seen equipment of this type, several System Engineers showed up to help conduct the test. Needless to say we failed. Even though we could establish the connection between UCLA and the Lab, we were not able to get the terminal to send data and receive output back to our site. After a frustrating afternoon everyone left and the CE and I went to dinner. About 7:00PM I got back together with the CE. I had prepared several test programs to send to UCLA. I put the cards in the reader and pushed the transmit button and the terminal began sending the data to UCLA. When the last card cleared the reader, the printer came alive and began printing the output for the test programs. What a relief, this connection would save us the long drive to UCLA. We would soon be able to communicate with the UCR computer center which would also save us from the constant running back and forth to the campus which was located about 2 miles away. The computer systems at UCLA were IBM 360, 75 and an IBM 360 50. These computers seemed large and fast to us but by today's standards these systems were very large, relatively slow and had limited online storage capacity.

Soon after we got our terminal working, UCLA CCN upgraded to an IBM 360 91. This was the largest IBM 360 ever built. The computer had 8 million bytes of memory which in the 1960's was unheard of. The size of the computer was impressive as it took up a room about the size of a football field. The computer was also water cooled and problems would arise when the system would spring a leak under the sub floor. Just finding 500 gallons of distilled water was a major challenge for the computer operations staff.

Following the installation of the 2780 terminal, UCLA and other California educational institutions began working to establish the California Educational Computer Consortium m(CECC). Since I was one of the few people around with good data communications background, I was invited to become an active member of this organization. The objective was to give all the colleges in California access to state of the art computer systems using data communications.

As things returned to normal, I began getting assignments from other projects at the Fire lab. Good programmers were hard to find and I was starting to get a reputation for being a good programmer who could solve most problems. One of the researchers, Ross Carter, was working on a concept of being able to build a fire modeling program. The model would require map inputs with fuel types terrain drainage channels etc. Ross had a technician coding different variables on a map. These variables were then entered on punch cards that would be entered into the computer when a program was written. I got the task of writing the program and soon we were able to display maps of an area with different attributes overlaid. The program was successful enough that we were able to publish the results of the study and for the first time I saw my name appear in print. The publication was a PSW research paper titled Informap, by Story, Carter and Tolin. It is still available in the PSW library.

The next assignment was a big challenge. There was a need to develop an automated dispatch program. The program would need to keep an inventory of available firefighting resources by location. It would be able to route the resources to a fire taking the shortest possible route, The program had to take into consideration things like time of day, and terrain. Time was required as a fire truck could get caught in rush hour traffic. Terrain was important as a truck loaded with water would travel a lot slower going uphill and faster going downhill. I started the project by trying to locate a basic transportation program that could be modified to meet our needs. I came up with no references so I began the task of trying to develop the program. I think that this was one of the most frustrating jobs that I have ever had. Trying to figure out how to route a fire truck through a maze is not an easy task. For several months, I would come to work and work all day trying to figure out the logic of how to get through the highway network without backing up. Every day I would start a logical sequence and work 8 to 10 hours. Sometimes I would think that I had the problem solved only to discover later in the day that the logic was seriously flawed.

One afternoon, I was able to logically work my way through a highway network and in going through the logic several times, I could not find any logical flaws. This was exciting, I took my logic charts and wrote a computer program. I went to the keypunch and punched the code into IBM cards. I was scheduled to work that night at Riverside Community College where I taught computer lab. I got there early and fed the program into the computer. The answer came back almost instantly. I looked at the program output and I was convinced that the answer was incorrect. To make sure, I got an adding machine and worked my way through the network manually. To my surprise, the answers were correct. The visual inspection of the highway network made the computer output look incorrect but the actual travel times through the network were the fastest. The engine to find your way through the highway network was only the beginning of the program. Data bases had to be built to house the fire equipment inventory and the highway segment information. The other part that was far more complex, was finding a computer that could work on the problem in real time. In the 1960's most computers were strictly batch oriented. Time on these computers was very expensive. Finding a computer where we could enter fire coordinates and have the computer give us an immediate response was a major challenge. Personal computers did not exist. The only alternative was to use a timesharing service. Timesharing in the 1960's were large computers in a central location where users could call in using a teletype or a small typewriter like terminal. These terminals operated at 10 or 12 characters per second. We located 3 different timesharing services and began testing them to see if they could meet our requirements. We finally selected a service, Allan Babcock. The only problem with this was that the program models needed to be converted into Programming language 1 (PL1) by IBM. Just before I started the conversion, a transportation engineer from our Berkley Office gave us a visit to learn more about our transportation program. This engineer had uncovered a program written at Harvard and our engineer friend wanted to find out which program was the most efficient. I went to Berkeley and ran benchmarks on the UC Berkeley CDC 6400 computer. The Harvard model won out so with reluctance, I replaced my transportation program with the Harvard model. I then converted the entire program to PL1 and put the programs up on the Allan Babcock system.

Having completed the programming process and finding hardware to run the programs on, we needed to find a site where we could run the programs and dispatch real fire equipment. We selected the California Division of Forestry (CDF) central dispatch site in

San Bernardino. Once the program was up and running, we made a press release. Articles about the new system appeared in the Los Angeles Times, San Bernardino Sun, The Riverside Press Enterprise etc. I will never forget the headlines in the Los Angeles Times. It read "Big Rookie, kind of good and kind of slow". Even with the timesharing computer, it took 2 or 3 minutes to make a dispatch. State Fire dispatchers were expected to have equipment starting to roll in less than 30 seconds. The other problem uncovered during the test was the cost. Phone charges and computer time to run the program cost a few thousand dollars a month and it was just not practical to put into everyday use. We were able to publish the results of our study in a National Magazine, Fire Control Notes. I also got a big write up in the in computer magazine of the 1960's DATAMATION. A few years later an employee of mine, Martin Wefald would develop a working program on an Apple PC. This program would not only track fire equipment on the ground but would also track aircraft. Apple computers were affordable and soon became a standard fixture in Region 5's dispatch centers.

In the 1960's using a computer in fire camp would be a large asset. The problem was that computers were too large to have in fire camp and had too many special environmental requirements. We again got the idea of using a timesharing service. The problem with this idea was that we would need to be able to use phone lines that were reliable. This could be a challenge in the 1960's. There were a lot of Mom and Pop phone companies around and nobody seemed to know if these telephone services could support a connection to a timesharing service. We decided to test the phone lines to see if we could make a good enough connection for a fire camp. Our tools for this was an IBM typewriter terminal and an ASR 33 teletype. Since we did not know if electrical power would be available at remote sites, we added a gas powered generator to our inventory of tools. Our test took place on the San Bernardino National Forest. The test was simple, all we needed to do was drive to different points on the forest and find pay telephones. Once a pay phone was located, we would stop, hook our computer terminal up to the pay phone using a cradle type computer modem. The terminal and modem were then connected to our portable generator. Using out telephone credit card, we would call a timesharing service and test programs inputs and outputs. We had a success rate of about 75%. We found out that we could either get the connection to work or fail. There was no in between.

As time passed, I continued to work with UCLA Campus Computing Network. The objective was to develop a process that would allow a terminal operator at a remote site to control computer run streams. Imagine a situation where a programmer accidentally developed a program that printed page after page of worthless output. How could you stop your printer and tell the computer mainframe to cancel the print job. UCLA developed a program called RJS that would give remote batch terminal operators the same control over their card readers and line printers as they would have at the main computer site.

In early 1969, the station Biometrician, Bill O'Regan told me that in order for me to advance my career, I would need to finish my education and get at least a masters degree. If I did this and worked hard, I could get promoted to a GS 12. He ask me what I was going to major in? I told him that I wanted to major in Computer Science. Bill told me that Computer Science was unacceptable and that I would need to focus my education in the area of biometrics. This was quite a let down and I began thinking about leaving the Forest Service. I seemed to have reached a dead end job that would allow me to work with computers and remain at the GS 11 level for the next 20 years. This was not much to look forward to.

There were interesting things going on at the Lab. A friend of mine was working with Monsanto to develop a new fire retardant that would be used with the air tankers. They came up with using a Diammonium Phosphate jell. A form of this is still being used today. It is a vast improvement over the borate that was used when I worked at the Chino airport. The mix is a fertilizer. The drawback is that Diammonium Phosphate is very corrosive and will slowly erode the airframe on the retardant aircraft.

I started looking around for a new job. I applied for government jobs in Hawaii and at Edwards Air Force Base. The word must have gotten out because I got a call from my boss in Berkeley who told me that there were job openings in Washington DC. He urged me to apply for one of the vacant jobs. I took his advice and applied, fully expecting to be turned down. About a month after I sent the application in, the Lab Administrative Officer came to my office and told me that I had been selected for one of the Washington Office jobs and Washington wanted to know how soon I could get there. I responded that I would be there in about a month. I then took the rest of the day off and went home and downed the better part of what was left in a bottle of bourbon. I left the Fire Lab at the end of September and reported to my new boss in Washington. Oh yes, I got promoted to a GS 12 without the fancy biometrics degree.

PART III:
THE WASHINGTON OFFICE A
NATIONAL PERSPECTIVE

Project Inform

Computer Science

Ft. Collins Computer Center

Houston Space Flight Center

INTRODUCTORY COMMENTS

On a Wednesday late in September, I took our family car to the train station and arranged to have it shipped to Washington DC. The price was fairly reasonable only $400.00 for a low priority shipping. This would save the government money for our transfer. The next day the movers showed up and loaded the van with all our possessions. Late in the afternoon the moving van left for Washington DC and we left Riverside for my father in laws house. It was a sad departure, both of my boys were crying and our family cat was having a fit. My wife looked at me and said can you imagine driving all the way across country with all of this going on? The move was very hard to do as we were giving up a very secure living arrangement and heading into an unknown world. I had visited Washington DC when I was 11 years old and had memories of what it was like but I had no concept of what it would be like to live and work there.

The next day, my father in law took us to the Ontario airport where we caught a commuter flight for Los Angeles International airport. In Los Angeles, we boarded an American Airlines 747 that was headed for Washington Dulles airport. The 747 airplanes had just started flying and they were equipped with a lot of creature comforts, including a piano bar at the rear of the aircraft. We left for Washington DC in a 747 that was about ½ full. In those days most flights were not filled to capacity. My oldest son Bryan found himself a window seat soon after the plane took off. Youngest son Barry amused himself playing with the stewardess call buttons.

We arrived late afternoon at Dulles airport. I rented a car and we found our way to a motel in Alexandria Virginia. The motel had been arranged for by our realtor who would find us temporary quarters to stay in until our house in Riverside got sold, giving us enough money for a down payment on a new home. On Saturday morning, we met our realtor and he showed us several houses that were available to rent. We selected one in Fairfax VA. The realtor then took us to the District and gave us a little tour of where everything was. He showed us the South Agriculture building where I would be working. He told us that before the Pentagon was built, that the South Agriculture building was the largest building in Washington DC.

Early on Monday morning, I took the bus from our motel in Alexandria to Washington DC. The bus dropped me off right in front of the South Agriculture building. With a little bit of luck, I found the Computer Science Group (GSG) located in the 4th wing of the building. When I entered the CSG office, there didn't appear to be anyone there. I noticed that there was a very awkward looking word processing machine in the office and I moved closer to have a look at it. In 1970 word processing was not widely used and a clerk typist who could type error free pages were well paid and in high demand. As I moved towards the word processor, a person in the next office, saw me. It was Hobby Bonnet, the Branch Chief for CSG. Hobby seemed glad to see me and he confirmed that I would be working for Project Inform. Hobby also told me that he had convinced my new boss, Tom Jones, to let me work on a special project for CSG for two or three weeks. It seemed that no one in the CSG had any experience with timesharing systems and Hobby wanted me to look into getting a timesharing system for the Washington Office. Hobby had to leave the office that day to go to a training session but he turned me over to one of the staffers, Ron De Clark. Ron took me downstairs where there was a bus which he told me ran every 30 minutes between Rosslyn Virginia and the South Agriculture building. Ron told me to go to the 7th floor of the office building located at 1621 N Kent street and report in. He said that when I got done, to come back and he would show me around. The personnel officer that I saw got all the paperwork for my transfer together. He gave me forms to fill out and return at a later time. He also ask me why I hadn't taken a house hunting trip? I told him that it was my understanding that you either got a house hunting trip or temporary quarters. He told me that this was bad information. The subject then went to the shipping of the family car. I had understood that this would be at my own expense. I was told to put in for it as traveling the way I had was far cheaper than driving across country. This would be a bonus that I really needed.

I took the bus back to Washington and got back with Ron. He took me on a tour of Computer Sciences including the operations section. He also introduced me to the Project Inform Staff and my new boss Tom Jones.

At 11:00 AM Ron and a couple of other CSG employees got together and we all went to lunch. This turned out to be quite a lunch as it lasted until about 4:00 PM. We started with food at a restaurant in the L'Enfant Plaza. Then things started going down hill as we migrated from one bar to the next. The favorite drink that everyone else was having was called a blue diamond. I just stuck to beer. We got back to the office at about 4:20 and soon after I caught the bus back to my motel. On the way I remember a sort of panic setting in as I knew that I would never be able to afford the lifestyle that I had just been exposed to.

THE JOB

I began the task of putting together a small study that would allow the CSG to acquire a timesharing service. I did all my writing in longhand and I soon found out that there was no one available to type the report. I felt that my first Washington Office project should look somewhat professional and as the study neared a conclusion, my wife typed it up for me. I recommended that we get General Electric Timesharing. The irony of this was that the person who had supported the Fire Lab account had been transferred to Washington about the same time as me. She would be our new account representative. A few people took interest in the timesharing system but after about a year we discontinued the service due to the lack of interest.

Having completed the timesharing study, I reported to Project Inform. I liked to refer to my new boss, Tom Jones, as the singer. Tom told me that the reason I was picked to come to Washington was the vast experience that I had with automated mapping systems. This made my blood run cold. Sure, I knew what a road map was and I had used topographic maps in the Boy Scouts and the army. Sure I had written a very simple program at the Fire Lab for a couple of researchers but they knew what they wanted and the model was well defined and very simple. I was stuck and began trying to find out what the folks in Project Inform wanted for a geographic locator system. To make things worse, the lead analyst for the project Phil Haug, had some very strange suggestions. One was that I should think of the world as a very large spinning disk drive. All that I needed to do was figure out how to read the data. Phil loaded my desk with lots of reference material. He introduced me to the mapping specialist in the Engineering office. The harder I worked at trying to find out what the Forest Service wanted the more confused and frustrated, I became.

The job did have a few perks. I contacted the US Army Topographic Command. They invited me down to view their systems. One of the most interesting systems was the simulator that the army had developed to assist astronauts with their moon walks. The concern at NASA was that a person could easily get lost on the lunar surface so the objective was to get the astronauts familiar with the area they would be working in. I got to go inside the simulator which was using a model that had been developed for the last moon walk. Once inside the simulator you would swear that you were on the moon's surface. The model was complete with landmarks, small rocks, dust etc. Needless to say I was very impressed. Next, I took a look at the types of software that the army used in the topographic command. They had several packages that I felt would meet the Forest Service needs. The problem was the software was classified and the army wouldn't declassify it so we could use it. Back to the drawing board.

The primary objective of Project Inform was to build a very large Information System. The concept was the Chief of the Forest Service or one of the top managers could go into a war room type atmosphere and locate valuable natural resources or combinations of those resources. Thus the need for a geographic locator along with the need for a very large and sophisticated data base management system. Phil Haug had taken the lead for getting the data base management system (DBMS). The procurement had been a competitive one and the TRW GIM system was selected. Once the selection was made, a competitor for the DBMS, sued the Forest Service stating that we had made the incorrect selection. Project Inform came to a screeching halt while the lawyers and a Federal judge sorted out all the arguments. After several weeks, the Judge ruled in the Forest Service's favor, stating that the law suit was the product of a poor loser in a competitive federal procurement.

I began working with the Forest Service mapping experts in the Geometronics section. They introduced me to the H DELL Foster digitizer. Using this tool, a technician could digitize layers of map information. In theory, multiple layers could be over laid thus creating a picture of selected combination of resources. Apparently I was the guy that the Forest Service was counting on to develop the software. Using the H DELL Foster, was a slow and tedious process. The ability of the digitizer was very limited and if you used a plotter to plot out what had been digitized, you could see the very rough edges from the unsteady hand of the digitizer operator. To complicate matters, the digitizer was located on the 11th floor of the Rosslyn Office building and every time a plane passed over on its way to National (Regan) airport, the vibrations would show up in the data. This form of digitizing was very slow and painful.

In January, I got my first performance evaluation which was very generous. I wondered what I would need to do to continue receiving good ratings. As it turned out, I didn't have to wait very long. In late March, Tom Jones and I were in a meeting with the Engineering staff. The main issue of the meeting was that Engineering wanted to purchase better digitizing equipment. They also wanted each of the Forest Service Regional Offices to purchase digitizers from the same contract. Near the end of the meeting, I made sort of an off handed remark, saying that if Engineering needed a Request For Proposal

(RFP) written for the purchase of digitizers, that I would be happy to do it. Someone made the point that the procurement would need to take place during the current fiscal year which ended on June 30. I told them that I didn't see a problem in getting it done. My boss, Tom, was not looking too good and when we got back to our office, he sat me down and ask me if I were serious about the procurement. I told Tom that if I could have the people that I wanted on the team that we would get it done. This was a high risk on my part as the Forest Service had never been able to get a large scale procurement in the data processing field, through the Department of Agriculture and the General Services Administration (GSA).

Tom, greased the skids for me and I named my team. The people that I wanted were: Randy Vangelder who I had worked with in Riverside, Kay Gonsier the project secretary from the Riverside Fuel Break Project, Jim Hogan, Washington Office (WO) Engineering. The other person who would sit in and provide periodic help was Olin Bacus from the WO Geometronics unit. In Mid April the team met. The challenge was that we needed to have the RFP completed in two weeks or less. Kay was the lifesaver as she took great shorthand and her typing was always perfect. We would sit in the Engineering conference room and figure out the necessary specifications and then dictate them to Kay. At lunch time, Kay would type a draft for us so that we could review our progress right after lunch. In about four days we had the technical specifications ready to go to contracting.

Jay Hess was our Forest Service Contracting Officer. Jay put the legal boiler plate on our RFP and I proceeded to set up a meeting with the USDA Office of Information Systems (OIS). We would need technical approval from OIS and then the document would need to go to GSA for procurement authority. Hank Baur was my contact at OIS. We met with him for a couple of hours. Hank made a couple of minor changes to our specs and sent us to GSA. We got GSA approval in a couple of days which was absolutely amazing as this rarely happened. All in all, the drafting of the specs and getting the necessary approvals took only 9 days. While this was going on, the Regions were committing money to the project. During the 9 day period, about 5 million dollars was collected. I was holding my breath, could we get this procurement advertised and awarded before July 1. The clock was ticking.

The RFP was advertised in the Commerce Business Daily and the closing date for prospective vendors was June 1. This would give my team 1 month to evaluate the vendor responses and award the contract. If we failed, the Regions and the Washington Office would lose five million dollars and my career would most likely be over.

At bid opening, there were only two bidders, CALMA Graphics and Auto Trol. We were able to evaluate the responses and make a contract award in about two weeks. The contract was awarded to CALMA Graphics. The problem was that as soon as the award was announced, the losing vendor filed a protest stating that our technical specifications were not realistic. The protest was reviewed by GSA and the Forest Service evaluation and award was upheld. Needless to say, several people in the Washington Office took note of my accomplishment and soon after the contract award, I was promoted to a GS 13. I had never dreamed that I would reach this level in government. A GS 13 was the grade that my former boss Lisle Green had been and he would retire years later at that grade level.

Soon after the new contract for digitizers was awarded, I began to get some breaks of finding a way to satisfy the Forest Service geographic information locator requirements. I met a person from Redlands

California who was specializing in analyzing geographic information. His name was Jack Dangermond and he offered to sell us his software for $10,000.00. I liked the idea but could not sell the idea to my boss. Ultimately, Jack would develop a computer system called ARC/Info which would become a state of the art geographic processing system in the 1990's.

A few weeks later, a person from our Region 1 office in Missoula, Montana was visiting our office. He told me about a program that he was using called "COM LOOPS". The program sounded like it might meet our needs. I converted the program to run on the USDA IBM 370 and we made some benchmark runs. Our conclusion was that the COM LOOPS software would be a good engine for the Forest Service geographic locator. Once we had some working software, we put together a couple of contracts to develop the system further. We awarded the two contracts and work began on the new system.

A few weeks later, I was transferred back to the Computer Science Group and I would be replaced in Project Inform by a person from the Pentagon who had a different idea about what the geographic locator should be. A couple of years later, I would be asked to help fix the mess he got us into.

My new job in the CSG would be a major challenge as my predecessor had been in the process of developing an RFP for the Forest Service procurement of computer systems which it was calling remote batch terminals. The Department had reluctantly agreed to send the RFP to GSA for procurement authority. The first week back in the Branch, I got a good briefing on the RFP that had been developed. I also got introduced to my new staff which consisted of Marvin Storey a communications person from the Forest Service, Linda Diaz from the Army, and Jim Perry from the Pentagon. We referred to this group as the Technical Services Section. I began sifting through the RFP and discovered that it was a real mess. The author had not done a good job of organizing the document plus he had a very poor command of the English language. Soon I got a call from Hank Baur in the Department telling me that GSA was on its way over to discuss the RFP. When GSA arrived, we spent the afternoon listening to its representative who told us he had just a few picky comments about the RFP. He could have saved us an afternoon by just saying this document is junk, start over. I got the message and got ready to start working on a new RFP. Meanwhile, the Department met with my boss, Hobby Bonnet and told him in no uncertain terms that the Department would not allow the Forest Service to purchase computers. The Department did say that it would support the agency buying intelligent computer terminals.

I got together with my boss and we talked strategy. We decided to purchase small to very large sophisticated, intelligent computer terminals. We also decided to include in our RFP portable typewriter style terminals and semi portable computer terminals. My team went to work. We began organizing the intelligent terminal section of the RFP by defining 3 levels of remote batch terminals. The smallest terminal would basically be a card reader and a line printer. The larger level 3 system would have memory, some programming capability and would include magnetic tape drives which could be used for data storage. I also made work assignments to my team members to start developing specifications for the two interactive terminals that we intended to purchase.

It took us about 3 months to put all of this together. And I got in the habit of organizing a Friday luncheon with two purposes in mind.

First, I wanted my team to have an opportunity to relax and let their hair down. Second, I wanted to be able to meet with people who would help us expedite this procurement through GSA and the Department. I selected a well known Washington DC seafood restaurant, Hogates for the Friday luncheons. Hogates was an interesting place as occasionally you would see a famous astronaut or politician having lunch there. The word got out about our lunches. People would aggressively compete to get an invitation. The other thing that was really great was the price. In 1970's dollars we could get a shrimp omelet, plus the buffet plus a couple of drinks for about $10.00. We got well known as I always left a large tip for the waitress and there was always competition to wait on our table. One last note about the Friday lunch is that models from the local clothing stores would model during lunch. I would occasionally purchase a dress that a model was wearing and take it home to my wife.

After a long hard 3 months, the document was ready for the approvals. Since we had kept Hank Baur and Al Wilkerson from the department apprised of our RFP and gone over it with them during our lunches, the RFP literally flew through the department. It only took a few days at GSA and came back with the needed procurement authority. We advertised the procurement in the Commerce Business Daily and we estimated that the Forest Service would spend approximately 11 million dollars on this procurement.

The bidding ended and we had what we considered to be good bids for all three terminals. We recruited computer people from all over the Forest Service to come to Washington and evaluate the proposals. The evaluation took us about two weeks and we ultimately awarded the Remote Batch terminals to Data 100 Corporation which was located in Minneapolis Minnesota. Data 100 would ultimately become

Northern Telcom Corporation. We made awards for the other two interactive terminals and as we would find out later the semi portable terminal would be a disaster. The company for this terminal was Typograph and frankly we were victims of getting too much advice from the Forest Service user community. The Typograph terminal had too many features and never worked properly. To make matters worse the company went out of business about a year after contract award. The portable terminal was a big success. I don't remember who the manufacturer was but we were overwhelmed with orders, not only from Forest Service users, but from all the other agencies in the Department.

A few months after contract award, I again was promoted to a GS 14. WOW! In my wildest dreams I had never thought that I could reach this level within the government. Getting promoted required Department approval from the Secretary of Agriculture. As part of my promotion, the Computer Science Group was reorganized several additional functions came to me along with several more people. I was now in charge of all Forest Service Technical Approvals, National Computer Applications Development, Telecommunications and Washington Office Computer Operations which included the operations in both the South Agriculture Building and the Rosslyn facility. As more and more responsibility came to me I learned how to delegate to my subordinates and I took on a philosophy that the folks who worked for me were the best and that they might not do the job the same way that I would do it but it would be acceptable if the end product was well put together and was technically correct. In contrast, my boss, Hobby Bonnet, never let a letter go by his desk without making edits to it. This was frustrating to me and others who worked for him.

Early in the 1970's, the Department had taken the position that USDA was responsible for running the Department's large computer centers. At that time, the 3 main USDA computer centers were located in New Orleans, Washington DC and Kansas City. The Forest Service had built a very large building in Ft. Collins Colorado to house what was to be the Forest Service Finance Office. However, the Department had taken on this responsibility and had transferred most of the processing of payments to its New Orleans computer center. This left a very large empty Forest Service building in Ft. Collins.

Shortly after we got the terminal contract awarded, USDA approached the Forest Service and offered to put in a computer system for the Forest Service. The computer would be located at the Ft. Collins site and be run by the Department. Although the Forest Service would be the primary user, other USDA agencies would use the facility. Ultimately a Univac 1108 was selected for the Ft. Collins Computer and I received the assignment of working with USDA to get this center up and running. Many of my responsibilities included site preparation which called for getting the proper air conditioning, sub flooring, electrical power backup and fire suppression including the installation of a Halon gas system. Halon is an agent that effectively removes oxygen from the atmosphere in confined areas like a computer room. It is more expensive than a conventional sprinkler system but if the system is ever needed, the computer equipment will not be ruined by being sprayed with water. Also Halon does not conduct electricity which is very important in a large operational computer center.

I also got the task of providing input to the department about the computer configuration that would be required. Since the Forest Service would be the agency that would purchase the equipment, we were given a lot of leeway for selecting equipment for the new site. Later, I would have lots of arguments with the Computer Center Director, Dr. Cooper, over how the random access disk storage would be used. This is an argument that I would never win. I wanted to have the capability of users being able to call for the mounting and dismounting of their own individual disk packs. Dr. Cooper was against this and the only way a user would be able to have a dedicated disk pack was for that user to commit to leasing a dedicated disk drive on an annual basis. This was a very expensive alternative.

Ultimately the Ft Collins computer center got built and the computer and necessary support equipment was put into operation. This by its self had a major problem. The Forest Service is spread across the 50 states with 9 regional offices and several Forestry experiment stations which are spread throughout the country. While we were busy getting the computer site ready and the new computer configured, we discovered that the telephone company, Mountain Bell was not willing to give us the dedicated telephone lines that we would require for our remote batch terminals to communicate with the new computer. The position that Mountain Bell took was that they had invested a lot of money to support the Forest Service Finance Office and that the Finance Office had never opened leaving the phone company with a large investment in voice equipment that would never be used. The communications person for the department was not helpful as he wanted to employ a different strategy of just tying the 4 USDA computer centers together with wide band telephone lines. This strategy would not allow the Forest Service to use is terminals with the Ft Collins Center. We considered all kinds of alternatives including building our own backbone microwave system. The microwave would take our data from Denver to Ft. Collins. At first this seemed pretty farfetched but because there is a National Forest, the Arapaho Roosevelt, which stretches along the front country between Ft Collins and Denver, we would not need to worry about land acquisition. When this came to the attention of Mountain Bell they agreed to give us a limited number of lines to access the new computer center.

Now for the problem of getting a staff to run the facility. The Department picked Dr. Tommy Cooper as the center's Director. Dr Cooper was highly qualified and nobody had a problem with his selection. The Department also picked the Deputy Director Phil Ladd. We all had problems with Phil's selection as his main qualifications were his close political ties up on Capitol Hill. We lost this argument. Also selected to head up the Centers Administrative section was Hank Baur. Years later, Hank would become the Director of the computer center. The remaining positions at the center were competitively advertised Department wide. I applied for several of the new positions as did most of the folks on my staff along with other very talented Forest Service people. Ironically, the only Forest Service person who was picked for a fairly low level job at the facility was the administrative officer from the Arapaho Roosevelt National Forest which was a local Forest office. The Forest Service was shocked but could do nothing about the personnel selection.

Finally, the center was up and running and the Forest Service began processing a large volume of its data through the center. The new Data 100 terminals worked well and all that was needed was the ability to connect our interactive terminals to the computer. Again the Department's communications person was not interested. Instead he urged us to use his wide band communications that tied the 4 USDA computer centers together. What he forgot was that with the exception of our Washington Office and the experiment station in

New Orleans, nobody else was close enough to access a USDA center. We worked hard on the problem and were finally able to scrounge enough telephone lines to build our own interactive communications network. To accomplish this we purchased CODEX multiplexers and modems. These were located at major Forest Service sites such as Regional Offices. The biggest problem that we had was with General Services (GSA). Our network would only be successful if we could provide toll free access to our multiplexer sites. Our plan called for getting this access by using the General Services FTS telephone network. To do this we would need approval from General Services (GSA). The problem was complicated by a person named Henry at GSA. Henry had been working hard to get government agencies to use FTS for data communications. The problem with Henry was that he had a hard time grasping our plan but we finally convinced him to give us the necessary approval. The Interactive network became a big success and the communications person at USDA became very jealous. Suddenly the Forest Service had a working network of high speed remote batch terminals that were complimented by a nation wide network of interactive demand terminals. What made the Department look bad was that they had the 4 department centers linked together with high speed communications but nobody used that network.

Now, for the big test. After about 3 months of successful operations the time came to run the acceptance test on the new Univac computer system. I was assigned the responsibility of putting the benchmark together and making sure that all the Regions would get their jobs successfully submitted to the computer. At this time in Forest Service history, the major computer applications were fiscal and accounting programs and a major application for designing roads. I coordinated with all the regions and developed the strategy of how we would submit the jobs to the new computer. Dr. Cooper and his staff were very confident that there was no way that the Forest Service could possibly use very much of the new computer's capability. Dr. Cooper estimated that the maximum use we would make during the benchmark run would be about 8 to 10% of the Univac's capability. What Dr. Cooper had forgotten was that a lot of the Forest Service applications were already compiled and resident of the Ft Collins system.

At noon we started running the benchmark nationwide. All the regions plus some of our Research Stations participated in the effort. Each Region had a tray full of run cards and job setups. The data and the programs had already been sent to the center and were resident on the computers mass storage. About 30 minutes into the benchmark, the Regions began calling me and telling me that they had sent all their computer run streams to the computer. I told them to keep resubmitting the jobs until I told them to stop. When Univac's operating system EXEC 8 saw a duplicate job being submitted to the system, it would automatically assign a new job number to the job being submitted. About 45 minutes into the benchmark, the Univac crashed and had to be rebooted. The Regions resumed submitting their jobs to the center. About 15 minutes later the Univac crashed again and had to be rebooted. At this point the computer had about a 7 day backlog of jobs to process. The center called me and requested that we stop sending work to the center. I called all the Regions and had them stop sending work to the center. About 3 days later, the center still had a major backlog of work and called me to see what should be done with all the output that had been generated. I told them it was only benchmark data and that they could just put all that paper in the trash. This led the folks at the center to ask the next question. Did they have to continue processing all those benchmark jobs. I gave the permission to abort the remaining benchmark runs.

A couple of weeks later, we rescheduled the benchmark and working with the Ft Collins staff agreed to only submit the run streams once from each Region. Even with this small amount of input it took the computer the better part of a day to work its way through the benchmark. For this test, I went to the computer center to observe. The Univac only crashed once during the final benchmark run.

As time progressed, we had a couple of major problems with the Ft. Collins Staff. The first problem started when we got a copy and analysis of who had been using the Ft. Collins computer during its first year of operations. Remember, that the Forest Service had paid for the procurement of the computer, all the site preparation as well as the salaries of the Ft. Collins Computer Staff for the first year of operation. It had been agreed that after the first year of operations that each Region and Experiment Station would pay for its use of the computer. Payment would be based on each users actual use of the system. What we discovered when we looked at the analysis was that the computer center had been giving a lot of free time to other USDA agencies. None of these agencies had ever put any money into the building or operations of the computer center. The Forest Service cried foul to the Secretary of Agriculture and the Secretary's Office agreed to reimburse the Forest Service for the system use by the other agencies.

The other major problem that I had with the center was that Dr. Cooper and his staff saw no reason why they should implement the Univac software that would allow the remote batch terminals to have control over their own run streams. From the centers' perspectives all that was needed was for the user to submit his job and the output would be delivered back to the remote terminal. This demonstrated to me that knowledge by the Ft. Collins staff was quite limited to computer centers where a user submitted jobs over the counter at the center and then would pick up his output at a later time. On the other hand, I had a lot of experience working in the area of remote batch processing. Much of this experience had been gained when I worked at the Riverside Fire Lab and the folks at the UCLA campus computer center (CCN). At one point early in my computer career, I had worked with Dr. Ken Tom and a systems engineer, Van Martin, at UCLA to develop a process that would allow remote users complete control over their remote terminal. At the Fire Lab, we were always doing computer program development . In a development environment a lot of things can happen and things go wrong with the program under development. One example is what is called a runaway printer. A runaway printer can be defined as a problem that occurs where the program that is being run goes into a print loop or has a problem with the printer carriage control characters with the end result that a single word, character or line of print would be printed on a single page of paper. Imagine what would happen if the output being generated was about 10,000 lines long. You guessed right, you would print 10,000 pages of output. At first you might just try to shut the printer off. That would work great until you turned the printer back on and it resumed printing one line per page again. In short, I wound up having quite an argument with Dr. Cooper and staff during what I called a we / they meeting. We being the Forest Service and they being the Department folks running the computer center. After nearly a full day of arguing why we needed control at the remote terminal end I finally mentioned the problem with the runaway printer. You could see the lights go on in the eyes of the computer center staff. They knew exactly what I was talking about. In short, I got my way and I left the meeting with a splitting headache.

Ft Collins became a major meeting place for the Forest Service. It had great meeting rooms, per diem was reasonable and there were super restaurants in town. One of the best Steak Diane that I ever had was at a restaurant called the Catacombs. About a year after the center went into operation, my old boss from Project Inform asked if I could help get the geographic locator system working. One of the contracts that I had let was to get the program converted to the Univac Hardware and make some significant improvement to the system. The person who had replaced me in the Inform project had come from the Pentagon and frankly he didn't know too much about information systems let alone what was expected from a geographic locator or information system. The contract that I had written had been awarded to Control Data Corporation and the programmer that had been assigned to the project became intrigued with being able to print little symbols on the map. Things like a tent for a camp ground, a bridge etc. Because of this not too much had got done and to make matters worse, my replacement had decided to make the process a fully interactive system. This was never the intent as the program required large amounts of data and running the program in demand mode or interactively would be far too costly. We went to Ft. Collins and met with the project manager from Control Data who was responsible for the project. He agreed to go ahead and get the program up and running on the Univac. The person who had replaced me still insisted that this was going to be an interactive system and after a few months and thousands of dollars down the drain my replacement left the project and went back to the Pentagon. The Geographic locator project died.

While in Washington, I had a fairly large staff to manage and along with it came the usual problems associated with managing people. The other problem was that the Human Resources (HR) Staff was little or no help. They often sided with a person who had become a performance problem. Maybe this is why folks say that government civil servants are a lazy bunch of bums that don't do any work. When you work for the Federal government and try to discipline an employee, you often run up against real barriers. Many of the barriers come from the HR Staff. A case in point was the employee that my boss had hired into an employee upward mobility program. My boss was always looking for deals that would allow him to get an extra person on the payroll. A person who would not count against our staff employment ceiling. I did get the opportunity to interview the candidates for a programmer trainee position. These people were typically lower grade employees who worked in places like the mailroom or were common laborers. I helped select a candidate who seemed like he might make it as a programmer. The one factor that had convinced me of this was that the candidate had taken it upon himself to go to night school and get some training. For purposes of this story, I will call this person Ray. The Forest Service set up an ambitious training schedule for Ray. By the time Ray finished the training the government would spend at least $100,000.00 on him. After approximately 1 year of training, it became apparent that Ray had not been able to absorb any of the training material. While in school Ray had been promoted from a GS 3 to a GS 5 and was up for a promotion to a GS 7. Ray's immediate supervisor came to me and told me that after a year of training that Ray could not write even the simplest program. I told him we needed to document this and I laid out a simple program for Ray to write. All the program required was for the computer to read a data card, add a couple of numbers together and print the card image and the result of the calculation. After two weeks Ray was not able to complete the assignment. Ray's supervisor and I made the decision that further training would not help and we removed Ray from the training program. We also withheld Ray's promotion to a GS 7. Ray filed a grievance and got a person from another USDA agency to represent him. His representative proceeded to tell me that I was being unfair and that anyone could write a simple Fortran Program. I gave the representative a copy of the assignment we had given to Ray and told him to have Ray write that program. That was the last I heard from Ray's representative. It was not the last that I heard about the matter. Ray continued with his complaint and the next thing that I knew, I was being given notice that I had discriminated against this employee and that I might be removed from office for discrimination. Specifically the charges were that I had removed Ray from training that would allow him to advance and that I had withheld his promotion to a GS 7. Frankly I was scared to death as it looked like my career was about to end. Before any action was taken, the complaint was sent over to the Secretary of Agriculture's office for review. The Director of USDA Personnel reviewed the case and came back with a very angry reprimand for the Forest Service HR Director stating, that Mr. Tolin was within his rights for withholding Ray's promotion and for pulling Ray out of training.

Ray was reassigned as a computer operator in my computer room that was located in the South Agriculture Building. When I would drop into the computer room, it was common to find Ray sleeping and a sign posted on the remote batch computer terminal telling users to feel free to submit their own jobs. I really wanted to take this on but decided to leave well enough alone as I didn't want to get into another confrontation with HR. A few months later I was just passing through my bosses office and someone mentioned that they had gotten a call about Ray's time card. It showed that he had worked a lot of overtime. Our timekeeper informed the person making the inquiry that there must have been a mistake as our records showed no overtime for Ray. Around income tax time a lady who rode in my carpool made a horrible discovery. In those days, the W2 forms were printed out and sent to the responsible staffs. My carpool partner was putting W2 forms in envelopes and suddenly discovered that one of her employees who was at a much lower grade was making almost twice what my carpool partner was making. This was turned over to our investigators and they found that 6 people were involved in a scam of putting overtime on their timecards. The scam worked because after everyone had signed the timecards a person in HR would take the timecards that were being sent to the payment center and would modify them for herself and a few friends. Guess what? Ray was one of her friends. There were 6 people who were involved in this scam. They were all fired and were tried in Federal court. Ray was one of the ones who was convicted. He was lucky as all he got was a few months in Jail and probation. The ring leader got 10 years in prison. To help pay the government back, all the money that had been withheld from these folks paychecks for their retirement plan was confiscated to help pay for the thefts. One lady in personnel who had been my personnel officer was one of the people who had been convicted. She lost her pension and she had worked for the government for over 30 years and was getting ready to retire. Since she had little or no money paid into social security her retirement plans after prison must have had to have been put on hold.

Because of the experience that I had gained with mapping systems and the contacts that I had made with the Army Topographic command, I was given the job of representing the Deputy Chief for Administration in the Forest Service Remote Sensing program. Engineering Geometronics represented the Deputy Chief for National Forest Systems. It is a little known fact that in the 1970's, the Forest Service had a small program going at the Space Flight Center in Houston. Their job was to explore and fund projects that would assist the Forest Service manage National Forest Lands. A few examples of things that can be done from outer space is that satellite technology can spot things like bug and insect infestations. Marijuana plantations are quite apparent as the landscape takes on a new appearance in a very short period of time. Examples are that water appears where it normally would not be. The plant its self gives off a unique footprint that can be spotted from satellites and U2 aircraft. Overall, using this technology can be very useful to managing the National Forest System. Our job on the Chief's advisory panel was to evaluate NASA proposals and recommend funding of projects that would be beneficial to the Forest Service. To assist us, the Geometronics unit had a staff of about 20 people stationed at the .Space Flight Center. I had many interesting experiences with this assignment. Much of it was classified and cannot be discussed. One experience that is not classified was one afternoon the project secretary's husband was a model maker for NASA. When you build models for NASA, they are full size and look like the real thing. One afternoon, we were taken to a hanger where a model of the Space shuttle was kept. On Television this vehicle does not look very large but the real thing is quite large especially if you get to go inside and explore. The one thing that really impressed me was the size of the cargo bay. When you are in the cargo Bay, it reminds you of a 747 without any seats. So you can get a feel for the overall size. The other thing that is in the hanger is what was called a zero gravity floor. The floor was designed to blow air through tiny holes. When active, an object would be placed on the floor so that they would tumble like they normally would when they are in outer space. The zero gravity floor and tumbling objects are used to train astronauts how to grab objects in outer space with the shuttles remote arm. Its interesting to note, the remote arm can only support a weight of 50 lbs. In outer space this doesn't matter too much.

As time went on, it was recognized in the Forest Service that there needed to be a greater focus placed on the entire area of Information systems and technology. A team was formed to look at Forest Service requirements and make recommendations to the Chief. The study took at least 6 months to complete and I was assigned to look at several aspects of Forest Service Information Processing. During the six month period, I was on the road most of the time, going from Region to Region looking at how they conducted business. I would then report back to the study team on my findings. I remember one time I called home and asked my wife to get me some money and meet me at Washington Dulles Airport late on a Friday night, This was in the era before ATMs were readily available. I also mentioned to her that I would be leaving early on Sunday Morning to fly to Missoula, Montana. My wife jokingly said "why don't you just borrow some money from your friends and go to a Laundromat to do your laundry. Needless to say this study took a lot out of me. The study finally came to its conclusion and it recommended that a new Associate Deputy Chief be appointed and that three new staffs be formed to handle the Forest Service Information Technology. The staffs were Computer Technology, Information Management and Computer Applications Development and Standards. These recommendations were approved and a major reorganization began. Everyone in the Washington Office and in USDA was urged to apply for the open jobs. Everyone including myself was guaranteed placement but if we had a specific job in mind we needed to apply for it.

I put together my resume and applied for the Director's position for Information Management or the Director of Computer Applications Development and Standards. I felt fairly confident that I would be selected for one of the two positions. If I didn't get selected for a Directors slot, I was sure that I would retain my current job in the computer hardware / operating system software area. I was wrong on all counts. With the exception of my old boss Hobby Bonnet, two new Directors from outside the Information Processing area were selected. Jon Kennedy an engineer from San Francisco was selected for the Information Management Job. Jon had limited knowledge of Information systems. Jim Space, a forester from State and Private Forestry, was selected to head up the Applications Development Staff. Jim's only experience in computer applications development was very limited experience in writing simple Fortran Programs. I lost my bid for my old position and was assigned as the Branch Chief for Information Management Data Base Design. This was truly a shock for me. Cal Smith who had worked for us in Ft. Collins was selected to take my old job and head up the new Hardware / Operating System Software Branch. In about two years, the stress from the job would wear Cal down and he ultimately transferred to the District of Columbia Police Department to work as an analyst.

Most of the positions in the new organization got filled but the Secretary of Agriculture got involved and told the Forest Service that it could implement the new organization but that the number of GS 14 Branch Chiefs would need to be reduced. The end result was that two GS 14 positions were eliminated. Ultimately, the Branch that I had been assigned to take over was combined with another Branch in the Information Management Staff. My new Branch became the Design and Operations Branch.

I went into my new job very depressed and the last thing that I was asked to do for Hobby Bonnet was to get USDA approval to purchase 3 micro computers that would be used for Research and Development (R&D) in the new Computer Technology Staff. The irony of this was that no one in the new staff knew how to get approvals for procurement form the Department and no one knew how to develop technical specifications for purchasing the new micro computers. I spent a couple of weeks working on this project and then reported to my new Staff.

I went into my new job thinking that I knew all there was to know about Information Management. After all, I had worked for Project Inform and had learned about Geographic Locators, and how to structure and manipulate large data bases. I soon found out how wrong I was.

My new boss Jon Kennedy had attended a training session on Information Management before he reported to the Washington Office. The course that he had attended was given by James Martin who at one time had been an industry expert in the area of data communications. Martin had also been an active employee with the IBM Corporation. Over the years, Martin had become an expert in the area of Information Management. His philosophy was simple enough in that he believed that information and data were valuable resources and should be shared between employees and be considered as property of the company or corporation. At that time, some companies had taken steps to create information czars who would control the collection of information, the storage of information and information standards. It was believed that Information was the most valuable resource of an organization. The problems associated with this were that people liked to collect their own information, not share it and of course there were no information standards.

To get me and the other Branch Chief together on the new philosophy, we were both sent to the James Martin course. Following the training, my next marching order was to purchase the MRI Corporation's data management software, System 2000 and get it installed on the Ft. Collins Computer. This became a problem as the USDA computer folks objected to the Forest Service purchase of System 2000. This was because the other 3 Department computer centers already had System 2000 up and the USDA officials felt that if the Forest Service wanted to use the software that they could use it on one of the other USDA computer sites. This was a long hard fight but I finally was able to convince the powers that be to let the Forest Service purchase its own copy of the Software. It was lucky for me that a couple of the folks that I had hired to work for the new staff had a lot of good experience working with System 2000 so we could hit the ground running. Little did I know at the time of the procurement that in a few weeks we would really need this software.

A couple of weeks later the Forest Service was hit with a major task called RARE II. This stood for the Roadless Area Review and was the second time in 3 years that the Forest Service had been asked to conduct this study. The study was to look at all the roadless areas in the National Forest System and make recommendations to the Congress and the President as to which areas of National Forest land should be put aside and protected as wilderness. This would preserve the land in its natural state and would limit access to the areas. The study would require that the public would be given the opportunity to comment on the proposed wilderness areas . This was a very emotional issue for a lot of different interest groups and opinions varied widely as to what should be done. I was told on a trip to Florida not to let people know that I was working for the Forest Service as there was a group of off road 4 wheel drive people who would most likely take their anger out on me if they knew that I was part of the study.

One day while all of this was going on, our newly elected President, Jimmy Carter, requested a meeting with some selected personnel from the Forest Service. The President wanted input on how we could cut cost and streamline government operations. I think that one of the reasons my name came up was that I had a reputation for knowing a lot about data communications systems system development and computer hardware. With the RARE II project going on I was swamped and frankly didn't have time to talk to the President that day. I started looking for someone on my staff to represent me. This was frustrating as everyone was very busy and no one seemed to be available. I finally had to send my secretary. Interesting as I never got any feedback on my decision to keep working on RARE II instead of meeting with the President.

RARE II had a lot of deadlines and thank God we had good reliable data communications with Ft. Collins. The project was getting very large very fast and frankly we did not have the work space to conduct the study. We moved our operations to the old Post Office Building in Salt Lake City and setup 24 hour operations. Even though my folks had motel rooms to go to a couple of blocks away, they would often sleep on the floor or if they were lucky there were some old couches that were used. Public input forms had to be scanned and in depth analysis had to be made in very short order. The biggest problem was getting the necessary computer turnaround from Ft. Collins. The second largest problem was getting the necessary programs written and debugged and installed at Ft. Collins. I remember one of my best programmers almost refusing to get on a plane for Salt Lake as he was not happy with the program that he had written and he wanted a couple more days to get the job done. My boss, Jon Kennedy said no, we had to go with what we had, I didn't know until we got to the airport if my star programmer would show up. I was relieved when I saw him get on the plane.

We got through the Rare II project and the new Wilderness areas were established. Literally tens of thousands of acres were set aside. No one was happy as the environmentalist didn't think we had done enough and all the other interest groups didn't feel that we had done enough for them. When it was all over, I put a couple of my people in for performance awards. The each got a small pay increase and a check for$1000.00. This made my prior boss Hobby Bonnett very angry as he felt that I had not recognized one of his people who had recommended scanner input for the public comment. His person had spent less than 40 hours at the office building his proposal. My folks had worked around the clock, slept on floors written programs and done the analysis which was the basis for the award. All in all we were looking at a couple of people who had worked about 3 months to make the program a success. I don't think that Hobby ever forgave me for overlooking his person.

Soon after the completion of the Rare II project, my boss, Jon Kennedy got the job of his dreams. He was promoted to the Regional Engineers position in the California Region, Region 5. Soon after, a new Director for the Data Management Staff would be named. There was a problem, however, the new Director could not report for about 1 year. The Associate Deputy Chief for Administration approached me and ask me if I would be willing to take the Director Position for a one year period. I agreed and was promoted to GS 15. To me this was absolutely incredible.

A couple of months later, a position opened up in Region 5 for the Director of Computer Science. The position was located in San Francisco California. I expressed an interest in taking that position but also knew that I would need to honor my commitment to Deputy Chief Haney and continue as the Director of Data management in the Washington Office. Ultimately, I was selected to fill the job in San Francisco and an interim Director took over that position for the coming year. As all of this was going on a dark cloud began forming over the California Region and the Pacific Southwest Range and Experiment Station. A lady by the name of Jean Bernardi had filed a law suit which ultimately turned into a class action law suit representing the women employees in California. I had known Jean when I worked at the Fire Laboratory. I knew that she had had a lot of problems with the Forest Service and its management. Jean maintained that the Forest Service discriminated against women and that women did not have an equal opportunity for advancement. It is true that at that time in its history, the Forest Service was predominately an organization that was dominated by men. There were several reasons for this. First and for most, very few women received degrees in Forestry and Engineering. These were the two dominant occupations in the Forest Service at that time. One other factor was that many women were not physically able to do certain types of work. A good example was, a lot of women wanted to become smoke jumpers. Many women were just not heavy enough to parachute out of an aircraft. The danger was that they could get carried way off course by prevailing winds and would land miles away from the targeted drop zone. Jean had always had issues with the Forest Service and the problem was that as usual, Human Resources staff failed to properly handle the case. The Forest Service felt that it could win the case but the US Attorney's office made the decision to enter into a consent decree. The result of this was that many folks who had spent most of their lives in the Forest Service would wind up losing their jobs or have their career paths frozen. I would ultimately become a victim of the decree several years later.

My last year in Washington had its ups and downs, one of my biggest problems was to try and get the Forest Service headed down the right track by establishing good data and information standards. Most people in the Forest Service resisted this and in hindsight I am not sure that this is a battle that can ever be won.

During the year my old boss Hobby Bonnet was replaced as the Director of Computer Science, I made a run at the job but was told that I needed to go to California and get some Regional experience. I was promised that in four or 5 years, I would get an opportunity to take that position. I felt really bad for Hobby Bonnet as he had been the main catalyst for building Forest Service Information Systems. To his credit he was the one person who had been able to help the service forge ahead in computer science. No one who followed him would come close to his achievements. Hobby was put out to pasture with a small staff and he quickly disappeared.

One of the last things that happened during my final year was that a move was made to try and combine the Forest Service, the Park Service and the Bureau of Land Management. The idea was that one agency could more effectively manage the land than 3 separate agencies. Forest Service and the Park Service have major differences when it comes to managing our natural resources. The Forest Service philosophy was to manage the land and make the best utilization of natural resources. The Park Service on the other hand was for preservation. For example, if a fire starts on a National Park, the Park Service most likely will let the fire burn. An example of this was a few years ago there was a large fire in Yellowstone National Park. The Park Service let it burn until there was a large public outcry. At the last Regional Forester / Directors meeting that I attended in Washington DC, the Chief ask us to go to Capitol Hill and talk to any congressmen that we knew to try and stop this effort. The calling was urgent because once the president stated the intent for the merger, we could no longer lobby our cause on Capitol Hill. I visited one congressman who had been a law clerk for my dad and expressed my concerns to him. Ultimately the movement died. Its interesting to note, that in 2009, this particular movement has come back to life. I guess we will see where it all goes.

In August of 1979, we sold our home in Fairfax Virginia and moved west to San Francisco. This time our kids were older and we had two cats that seemed to tolerate the trip and the 7 nights that they would have to stay in a motel. As we drove across the country, I was a little concerned as my new boss had told me at a meeting that we had attended in New Orleans, that I was a young man and should take a job in a different Region other than Region 5. His problem was that he liked the interim director who he had appointed and he wanted that person to be his permanent director of Information Systems. I wondered as the miles passed by what it would be like working for a person who did not want me onboard.

PART IV:
THE CALIFORNIA PACIFIC ISLANDS REGION

We arrived in California about 4 days prior to my reporting date. This would give us time to get moved into our new house. In Benicia. It would also give me an opportunity to think about some of the issues that would be confronting me when I began working in the Region. Of primary concern was my new bosses' comments to me at a meeting a couple of months earlier. He let me know in no uncertain terms that he was not happy with me coming to the Region. He liked his current Director Clyde Shumway and did not like the idea that Clyde was being forced to live up to his agreement with Deputy Chief, Doug Leitz. The agreement was that Clyde would work in the Region for a year and then take a Washington Office assignment. I would replace Clyde as the Director of Computer Science. My new boss had stated to me that I was young and that other opportunities would present themselves in the future. This was a very real concern on my mind and I almost wished that I had stayed in Washington.

Other complex issues facing me in the Region would be, finding adequate and timely resources to support the Land Management planning activities that were taking place in the Region. Congress had mandated that every National Forest develop a Forest Land Management Plan and Congress had also set specific timeframes that the plans were to be completed by. Region 5 had 17 National Forest and one special management unit, the Lake Tahoe Management Unit (LTBMU). My involvement in the process was to make sure that each Forest got timely access to the Ft. Collins Computer Center to run the required analysis for developing the plans. To assist the Forest with the planning process a linier program had been developed that would allow Forest planners to look at what would happen to the land under different management strategies. The name of the modeling program was FORPLAN and it required most of the resources available at the Ft. Collins Facility. To facilitate running this model. The Ft. Collins facility would become the largest civilian Univac computer center in the 50 states. The program took so many resources on the Univac that only 5 to 10 runs could be accomplished during the graveyard run. Region 5 Forest would be in competition with all the other Forest Service Regions for these Resources. To make matters worse, the Sierra Club did not like the idea of the Forest Service using models to look at impacts on the land under different management strategies. Sierra Club lawyers would show up at management team meetings and threaten legal action to prevent the use of FORPLAN.

My predecessor to the Region had allowed the purchase of mini computers (DEC PDP 1170s) on the National Forest without receiving the proper technical approval from the Washington Office. This had been a major concern when I was in the Washington Office and the issue would blowup shortly after my arrival in the Region. To make matters worse, my predecessor would later try to blame me for his actions.

Time passed quickly and my reporting day came. I took the BART train from Concord to San Francisco. It was a short walk from the train to my new office. I was very apprehensive about my new staff as I did not know if they would like me. My new boss was upset with my arrival in the Region. Both of my Branch Chiefs, Bill Fredeking and Tom Tokas, would become true friends and loyal supporters. I would manage a staff of approximately 45 people and have an annual budget of approximately 10 million dollars. I would soon find out that having such a large budget to manage was not an asset as the Regional Forester, Zane Smith, would always be challenging me as to why I needed such a large budget to run Computer Sciences. At 9:00 AM, I went down to the Regional Foresters office to let my new boss, Curt Smith know that I had arrived. To my surprise, Curt was on vacation and would be out of the office for about two weeks.

I returned to my office and arranged for each Branch Chief to give me a briefing on current projects that they were working on. Tom

Tokos reported that he was working on developing Forest Level data bases and was in the process of doing the analysis of information needs and flows. Tom was following a conceptual design that my predecessor Clyde Shumway had put together. From my experience at the National level I knew that the design was flawed and that we either need to go through a major redesign or abandon the project.

My other Branch Chief Bill Fredeking was in charge of computer operations and system engineering. Bill was a Forester by trade and was self taught in the Computer Science area. He would become one of my closest friends and professional advisors. As it turned out, both Bill and Tom were eager to work with me and we would work well together as a team.

The first two weeks passed quickly and I had my first official meeting with Curt Smith. Curt gave me two very specific orders at our meeting. They were: get rid of the Regions outdated CDC 3100 computer. It was expensive to operate and with the Data 100 terminals that had been purchased there was no need for a mainframe computer. With the DEC PDP 1170 mini computers the Region also had computing power at both the Forest Level and in the Regional Office. Curt also wanted me to reorganize my staff. Part of the reorganization called for me to take on the responsibility of all of the Regions communications systems. I was lucky as Curt assigned Tom Hensley to work with me on the reorganization effort. Up until the time that I came to Region 5, the communications function had been assigned to another staff, The Director of that staff was getting ready to retire and did not resist the reorganization effort.

I quickly became aware of two major personnel problems on the staff. The first one was in computer operations. The swing shift operator had a habit of calling in just before the shift change and saying he was sick or that he needed to take a vacation day. One of my staff members reported that this operator was a real estate sales person and that he would call in sick when he needed to show a house to a client. I sent a strong worded letter to this employee and informed him that he needed advanced approval before we would grant him vacation time off. He sent me a letter of resignation the next day.

The second personnel problem was another person who should have never been hired in the first place. Shortly after he had been hired his boss had uncovered the fact that he had lied on his application. This was grounds for terminating him but personnel had rushed to the persons defense and he had been kept on the payroll. I had his boss, Tom Tokas assign a fairly simple project to this person and we put his feet to the fire demanding that he produce a workable product.

After a few weeks this performance problem resigned.

It took about 6 months to get the last remaining programs off the CDC 3100 computer. My users were happy to get their applications converted to modern technology and I was lucky as the conversions went pretty smoothly. On the last day of the 3100 operation, the computer gave an electrical shock to the CDC engineer who was taking the computer off line. I guess this was the computers way of protesting its removal.

A couple of months after my arrival in the Region, I got a visit from one of the Regions personnel specialist. This person was responsible for all issues in the Region that dealt with safety. We discussed a lot of issues during his visit. One topic that came up was accident investigations. I mentioned that I thought it would be interesting to be an accident investigator. About a year later, I arrived at my office at the usual time of 6:30 AM. One of the reasons for the early schedule was that as a director, I would need to check with my counter parts in the Washington Office and make sure that there were no major problems or concerns in the information technology area that I was responsible for. I had just settled in with my first cup of coffee and the phone rang. It was personnel. They advised me that there had been a bad accident at the Heavenly Valley Ski Resort and they wanted to know if I was available to help investigate the accident. I replied that I was available but that I was scheduled for leave the following week and I wanted to know if being on the investigation team would interfere with my scheduled vacation. I was told that the investigation would take 2 or 3 days and not to worry. I would be able to go on my planned outing with my family. The information was wrong, I would spend the next 6 months working almost full time on the accident. My last question for personnel was who was the team leader and who would I be reporting to? I was informed that I was the lead investigator and that I should report to the Forest Supervisor at the Lake Tahoe Management Unit. I was also asked if I would like personnel to get me an airline ticket. I replied that I would be taking my own car. This would ultimately save a lot of time and money. I went home packed a bag and headed for Lake Tahoe. I told my wife that I would be home in a couple of days.

I arrived at Tahoe in the early afternoon and reported to the Forest Supervisor, Ralph Cisco. Ralph turned me over to his recreation folks who would fill me in on what had happened. They would also advise me of who else was on the investigation team. This accident had taken place at the Heavenly Valley Ski Resort. The resort was situated on Forest Service Land but was operated by a private company. The Heavenly Valley company had a special use permit with the Forest Service and paid the government for the use of the land. All the improvements to the property including the ski lifts and buildings were built and owned by the Heavenly Valley lift operator. In the case of major accidents such as the one I was about to investigate, there is a major concern that even though the US Government does not operate the facility, it owns the land that the facility is built on. The US Government is generally viewed in a case of this kind as "DEEP POCKETS" , meaning that in a law suite, the Government has unlimited financial resources and will most likely be the one that gets sued.

The Heavenly Valley accident had occurred during the early afternoon on a Sunday. The wind speed had been slowly increasing and the lift operators had been discussing the possibility of shutting the lift down because of concerns over the weather. The accident occurred on the "Ridge Chair (9)" when there was what is called a double de-ropement. In other words the cable supporting the lift chairs had come off of the lift in two places. Several people were seriously injured including A young lady related to Aleoto a prominent San Francisco person. Another victim was the niece of one of my employees. She had almost died at the scene but due to the skills of the Forest Service Ski Patrols First Aid she survived. Aleoto's granddaughter would be paralyzed from the neck down for the rest of her life. Immediately following the accident all persons who had been on the lift or close to it were interviewed by the ski patrol. Their names addresses and phone numbers were recorded before they were allowed to leave the mountain.

At the time of my assignment to the investigation team, I had no experience with ski lifts, did not know how to ski and I had never investigated an accident. I had originally thought that this would a training experience for me but as I was to find out soon, I would be the person responsible for the investigation. I was lucky, my team was made up of several experts. Gordon Linebaugh, who was the Regions Ski Lift Engineer. Bob Rice was an accomplished skier and a Forest Supervisor. Bob brought with him an accomplished person from the Mammoth Mountain Ski Patrol. A local Forest Service Ski Patrol person Sandy Hogan was also assigned to my team. Sandy was a real go getter and would advance her career in the Forest Service to a very high level. In less than 5 years, Sandy would become a District Ranger. She would continue the investigation on her own time long after the team had finished its work and Sandy would find additional evidence on the ground after the snow had melted. CAL OSHA joined us early in the investigation. These investigators specialized in accidents associated with rides in amusement parks. They were experts on equipment such as roller coasters, and trams, They were very interested in why the lift had failed.

The question on my mind was how does one without any experience go about investigating a major accident. Bob Rice proved to be a life saver in this area. He suggested that we develop some scenarios on how the accident might have occurred. We took the tram up the mountain and then took a snow cat to the site of the accident. We would spend several days at the accident scene and would go over the area with a fine tooth comb. We would climb up the lift to the rigging and carefully examine the cable catcher which was a device that had been designed to catch the rope in the event that it came off its track. The cable catchers had failed but why? Close examination showed where the cable had struck the cable catcher then for some reason the cable had come loose and was dropped by the cable catcher.

Following our trips up the mountain, we would discuss what we had seen and would work on developing possible causes of the accident. We were assisted by comments that had been made by some of the witnesses. One scenario we developed came from a witness statement about a couple of young skiers who were said to be swinging in their lift chair. Another scenario cited the weather and windy conditions. A very disturbing scenario was the fact that the lift had been modified during the off season. The modifications had been made without going through the proper Forest Service review approval and test procedures. Ironically the changes to the lift had been made in the interest of safety. A pylon had been moved to give skiers a safer path down a ski trail. Proper load testing had not been done. The Forest Service special use permit person had been aware of the changes but had not enforced the regulations.

During the first few weeks of the investigation, I would make daily reports on our progress to the Regional Forester and my old Boss in the Washington Office, Associate Deputy Chief Glenn Haney. Glenn had gained a lot of experience investigating accidents while he was my boss in the Washington Office. His specialty was aircraft accidents. Glenn gave me several good pointers on how to run the investigation. My weekly phone bill at the hotel would run into the hundreds of dollars and I am sure that the hotel enjoyed the profits that they made during the investigation. The Hotel manager rented me a conference room. Its location was kept secret as the news media was looking for us and any witnesses that we might be interviewing. It was interesting to me how the media reported this accident. We managed to keep the majority of witnesses away from reporters and the investigation team had virtually no contact with the press. In spite of this, we would hear and see news reports of the accident on TV, radio and in the newspapers. Most of the reports were totally false and had no true foundation.

As you have probably already guessed, the investigation was taking a lot longer than what I had been told at the beginning. I canceled my planned vacation and my family joined me for the Easter school break. They really enjoyed their vacation at Lake Tahoe. Several weeks went by and after a couple of months of living at Lake Tahoe, I would return to my office in San Francisco. Work on the investigation would continue for about four more months and the final report was presented to the Regional Forester and our attorneys. The findings concluded that it was the lift modification the summer prior to the accident that had caused the lift to fail. The distance between the pylons was to far and under the right conditions, including wind and load factors on the lift the deropment would occur. The Ridge chair (9) would be modified before the next ski season. I also made sure that ski ranger Sandy Hogan would get an outstanding award for her work during the investigation. A couple of months later, I learned that the law suits had been settled for an undisclosed amount. The Forest Service had not been named as a defendant and our attorney, Will Jennings told me that our team had done a great job and gotten the government off the hook for what could have been a very large payout by the tax payers.

Life for me returned to normal and the study to reorganize my staff had progressed during my absence. I had a great staff and they had done a lot of the required research and staff papers that would facilitate the reorganization. Total time for the reorganization study was about one year. When the study was completed, I would get the added responsibility for all the Regions communications systems including radio and telephone. I would also take over the Regional Directives system which supplemented the National Forest Service Directives System.

The Regional communications system would become the most complex part of the additional responsibilities that I would inherit. It included frequency management and monitoring all the radio and television stations that were on leased Forest Service land on top of Mt. Wilson. The big problem on Mt. Wilson was what we called frequency pollution. Keeping all these stations within their broadcast bands was a real problem. We would also get involved with international problems of frequency management. The problem was that our neighbor to the South, Mexico would begin using some of the Regions assigned emergency radio frequencies for simple things like taxi cabs talking to one another. Our only recourse was to complain to the State Department who told us that they would bring the topic up at the next meeting that they had with the Mexican authorities. The State Department ignored the fact that one of the primary areas that was being affected was our fire suppression teams that were responsible for protecting President Regan's ranch that was located near the Los Padres National Forest. The other major part of the communications activity was the construction of Forest Level microwave systems. Building the Forest microwave systems was a long and complicated process. It took an average of 5 years from beginning to project completion. The Region would spend about 10 to 12 million dollars a year on this project. To make matters worse, the Regional Forester had a bad habit of dipping into our money for some of his pet projects. I eliminated this problem by spending all our microwave construction funds on the first day of the fiscal year. To accomplish this, we would request proposals from the microwave vendors. The proposals would be evaluated and ready to award. On the first day of the fiscal year, the contracts would get signed. Later on in the year when the Regional Forester would go on his annual money hunt, he would try to tap our funds but to his disappointment he would find out that the money had already been spent.

You might wonder why we needed to spend so much on Forest level microwave systems. The problem in the 1980's was that our law enforcement people needed to have the ability to communicate with the outside world. Pot growers and gangs would hide out in areas where normal radios were unable to communicate. A law enforcement officer could get trapped by a gang member and have no way to communicate that he was in trouble. The same principal applied to fire suppression efforts and search and rescue. The end result was that the money for good communications was well spent.

We did have a major problem in the microwave area from one of our sister USDA agencies the REA. The REA had been formed in the early 1900's to assist people in rural areas with electrical and telephone communications. In the California Region there are still a lot of what we call a mom and pop telephone companies. General Telephone and Continental phone companies are just a couple of examples of small telephone company operations. The concerns by the smaller companies was that if the Forest Service built its own microwave networks, the smaller phone companies would get put out of business. REA sided with the small phone companies and showed up one day in the Regional Foresters office demanding an audience. Their lawyer would threaten us and try to intimidate us. I told them that I had no problem with them providing us with the service and to please give us a couple of weeks to put our requirements together. I set up a second meeting with them and invited our attorney Will Jennings to participate. The meeting opened with the REA and their client making demands and threats. They then noticed that there were several people at the meeting that they did not know. One of the representatives suggested that we all introduce ourselves. When Will Jennings introduced himself, the tone of the meeting changed. We were able to present our requirements. The problem that the phone company and the REA had was that they only wanted the easy part of the job. They did not want to staff up and give the Forest Service the 24 hour 7 day a week support service that was required. The support was especially necessary during the summer Fire Season. Since the issue was political in nature, the Washington Office got involved. They tried to curtail the development of Forest Microwave systems but were unable to come up with a viable alternative. Our microwave program continued.

I had been in the Region just over a year when the issue of the DEC PDP 1170 computers that Clyde Shumway had authorized came to the forefront. The issue surfaced because a California Congressman Pete Stark was in trouble and might have a problem in getting re elected. One of Pete's friends, a local newspaper reporter, came to Pete's assistance. He used the Forest Service as the vehicle to help Pete with his election campaign. This reporter went to the Plumas National Forest looking for issues within the logging industry. While on the Forest, he discovered that the Forest Service used computer systems to facilitate word processing and run computer applications. The reporter returned to San Francisco and wrote an article in the Chronicle saying that only at the NASA space flight center would you find sophisticated computer equipment like he had found on the Plumas National Forest. What he neglected to say was that the computer he was talking about was so small that it would fit in and average bedroom closet. Clyde Shumway who had been responsible for the purchase of the equipment, was now in the Washington Office. He pointed the finger at me but was unsuccessful as he had made this purchase while I was still in Washington. My Washington Office boss Glenn Haney was well aware of what Clyde had done and he moved in to help set the record straight.' This helped some but the article had gotten the attention of the General Accounting Office (GAO) and I got audited. For information, GAO is the audit arm of the US Congress. Normally, the auditors will do their best to find major problems to report back to the Congress. I was lucky, as the audit only took a couple of weeks and when the auditors were able to see live what the reporter had been talking about, they wrote it off. They also found that the computer that was referenced in the article was available to any federal agency and could be purchased using the GSA federal supply schedule.

During my first two years in the Region, the Washington Office had been working on developing a Request for Proposal to purchase mini computers service wide for every National Forest, every Ranger District and every research station. It was estimated that this procurement would cost approximately $100 million dollars. By the end of the contract period, this purchase would exceed $200 million dollars. As part of the procurement process, I would be invited back to Washington DC on a detail. The detail period would be for approximately three months and I would head up a team to evaluate vendor responses to the RFP. The detail its self was interesting. It started out with 3 vendors responding to the RFP. They were DEC, Data General, and Honeywell. Honeywell was quickly disqualified from the bidding as they were technically non responsive to the Forest Service requirements. Honeywell appealed to their congressional representatives but it was to no avail.

We proceeded with our evaluations and would spend two to three weeks at a stretch working out of the Rosslyn Virginia Office. I might add that there is nothing worse than being stuck in a place like Washington DC by ones self over the weekends. This is especially true if you had lived in that area for 9 years and had already visited most of the places of interest. On Sundays, some of the team members would get together for breakfast but after that the day would drag on. You would find yourself looking forward to going back to work on Monday. Finally after several months of flying back and forth to Washington, we would award the contract to Data General Corporation. The real challenge of getting all the equipment delivered and installed in the Region was about to begin.

The Regional Office which was located at 630 Sansome Street in San Francisco would be the first site for installation of the new equipment. This represented a major challenge for me as the building was quite old and was maintained by the General Services Administration (GSA). The new computers were designed to run using a series of interactive terminals. These terminals would need to be connected somehow to the mainframe which would start out to be one of two MV8000 computer systems. We selected a Local Area Network System that was manufactured by a company named "BRIDGE" The big challenge was to get the wide Ethernet cable installed in this old building. To do this, I contacted GSA and ask for their help. They politely told me that in two or three years they would be able to help us out. This time table was of no help as I had two or three months at the most to get the network installed and tested. In the 1980's, Ethernet net cables were thick, about 1 to 1 ½ " and would not tolerate sharp bends. GSA had told me that the cable trays in the building were full and I would have to use something else. I finally decided to take the ultimate risk to get my network installed. I knew from experience that GSA did not like politicians getting involved in their business. I picked up the phone one afternoon and called the chief building manager at GSA. IIe again told me that it would take two or three years to get the job done. I casually mentioned to him that this computer project had been sponsored by Congressman Phil Burton and would he like me to have the congressman contact him to see how we could get this project off the ground. That discussion was all that it took. GSA got moving and my LAN got installed in plenty of time.

The Data General computers that the Forest Service had purchased were state of the art in the early 1980's. The computers supported word processing as well as email. The internet was not yet ready to support things like email so the Data General equipment was pretty advanced for its time. Our first computers got delivered and installed in the Regional Office. In less than a year the entire office became 100% dependent on the system. The miracle of email surfaced, and the Forest Service was the only agency within the Department of Agriculture that had the capability. People would marvel at the fact that we could send an email with an attached document to anywhere in the Forest Service. We could send it certified and request a return receipt. You could be on the phone with a person in Washington DC and tell them that you had just sent them a document. You could hear the beep on the phone telling the recipient that the document had arrived. People from other USDA agencies from time to time would barrow a terminal so that they could communicate with their Washington Office. Within the first year, all the National Forest in the Region would have a Data General System installed. Within three years all the Ranger Districts would be installed and operational.

The limitations of the Data General equipment would soon become apparent. The original MV8000 systems were too small and too slow. Over my remaining years in the Region, I would move to replace the dumb computer terminals with what I called intelligent computer terminals. The intelligent terminals were micro computers (PCs) and we recommended that users buy either Compaq or IBM systems. This would get me into trouble with the Washington Office. Specifically, Clyde Schumway. Clyde did not believe that PCs were user friendly and therefore they should not be used. The user community in Region 5 disagreed with Clyde and years later when he thought it was his idea, he would admit that PCs were the way to go.

I had been in the Region for about a year when we got a visit from our Junior Forester who was stationed on Saipan which is an island in the pacific. I found out quickly that the Forest Service in Region 5 had a Pacific Island Forester who was stationed full time in Honolulu. Periodically he would visit certain islands in the pacific. These islands included, the Northern Marianas, Guam, Saipan and the Federated States of Micronesia including the islands of Pohnpei, Truk, Yap and Kosrae. The island of Palau was also included in the regions program. Our Junior Forester was stationed full time on Saipan and worked with the local residents on conservation projects aimed at restoring the islands natural vegetation and hardwood trees. During the briefing, several slides were shown depicting the Saipan landscape and I remember thinking to myself, wouldn't it be great if I could someday visit this place. Following the Junior Foresters briefing, the Pacific Island Forester, briefed us on some of the projects that were ongoing. The projects were aimed at restoring the islands to their native vegetative state following World War II. During the war many islands vegetation was destroyed by constant bombing and the dropping of napalm. Immediately following the war, some of the islands were seeded with grasses and other vegetation that prevented the natural re growth of the native species. To correct this problem, the US government established grants with the island governments to work on re vegetation projects that would restore the natural cover. The mission of the Pacific Island Forester was to monitor the progress of the re vegetation projects.

In the Spring of 1986, I got a call from the Pacific Island Forester, Len Newell. Len told me that the foresters and conservation people in Micronesia had requested that the Forest Service send a knowledgeable person to the islands to educate them in how they could put computer technology to work for them. For me this was the dream of a lifetime but I knew that the Regional Forester would most likely tell me to send a staff person.

I gave a lot of thought to whom I should send to Micronesia and decided to send my staff assistant Wendy Matyas. Wendy, had a background in education and was an accomplished computer person. I made the arrangements for Wendy to make what was to be a four week trip. During the trip she was scheduled to visit Pohnpei, Truck, Guam, Saipan, and several other islands. Needless to say, I was green with envy. Wendy left and had been gone about 4 weeks when I got a message that she was stuck on Pohnpei. The problem was that the island government had made a decision to rework the main runway at the airport. After they had torn the runway up it was determined that the repaving equipment that had been left following the war no longer worked. The result was that all work on the runway stopped until parts for the repaving machine could be located. This created another problem, namely commercial aircraft could not land on the island. Several weeks went by and Wendy appeared to be stuck. Finally, a small aircraft was brought in and flew Wendy to another island where commercial service was available. Wendy returned to the Regional Office with a lot of great stories to tell us.

A few months later, I got another call from the Pacific Island Forester. He wanted to know if I could accompany him on a trip to Micronesia. The main purpose of the trip would be to work with the Federated States of Micronesia on communications problems that were quite prevalent on the islands. I told the Pacific Island Forester, Len Newell, that I would love to go but that I would most likely have problems getting the Regional Forester to approve my taking this trip. Len told me that he would convince the Regional Forester to let me go. A couple of weeks later, I got called down to the Regional Forester's office. The Regional Forester, Zane Smith, showed me a letter from the Secretary of Agriculture of the Federated States of Micronesia. The letter requested my assistance to help the island government resolve communications problems. Zane ask me to coordinate my visit with the Pacific Island Forester and directed me to give whatever assistance I could to the island government.

Wow, it looked like my dream was coming true. I began getting emails from a friend of mine, Ed Petties, who was employed as a Forester for the State of Hawaii. Ed had been detailed to work with the Federated States Government for a year. He would be going with me and Len on our trip through Micronesia. I was getting the emails and bringing them home. My wife, Myrna was reading them and she was letting me know in no uncertain terms that she wanted to go with me on this trip. I was reluctant at first but finally gave in and ask Len if Myrna could go. Len said it would be ok but that some of the areas we would be visiting would be quite primitive and that if primitive conditions bothered Myrna, she should stay home. I told Len that Myrna and I did a lot of camping and that she would be ok. I ask Len to make Myrna's airline reservations and also make arrangements for me to pay for her airfare. Prior to leaving, I was told that it was tradition for high ranking officials who visited the islands to bring simple gifts for the people they would be visiting. I purchased a small case of Forest Service hats that had been designed by my communications people. The hats were a bright blue and had the Forest Service Shield on the front. A lighting bolt went through the shield and just below the shield were the words Region 5 communications. Little did I know how big a hit these hats would make with the local natives.

In early September, Myrna and I boarded a flight for Honolulu. That evening, we watched the sunset over the pacific and speculated on what our trip would be like. We left our hotel at about 2:30 AM and headed for the airport. We found the Air Micronesia ticket counter which was quite small. We were lucky, we were the first ones at the counter and this would afford us the best seats on the airplane.

Air Micronesia is owned by the Federated States of Micronesia. In 1987, the airline was flying Boeing 727 aircraft which had a very unique seating configuration. About ½ of what would normally be the passenger compartment, was used for cargo. Separating the passengers from the cargo was a cargo net. Because we had been the first to check in, we had been assigned to the best seats that had the most leg room. Since we would be on this aircraft most of the day, the extra room was appreciated. One last detail about this flight was we would be landing on some islands that were highly classified and if you did not have the proper paperwork, including passport, and security clearances you didn't get on the plane. If you were on the plane and were not cleared for a particular island, you would not be allowed off of the plane.

As we were boarding the plane, we noticed that a maintenance crew was in the process of changing a couple of tires that had apparently blown out during the aircrafts landing. After boarding, a couple of hours went by and then came an announcement that one of the aircrafts navigation devices had malfunctioned and we were waiting for the replacement unit to be installed. Another hour went by and then we enjoyed our breakfast sitting on the ground waiting for the necessary repairs. Finally we took off and flew for a couple of hours to the Sun Atoll. In 1987, the Sun Atoll was a place where the United States was working on a safe way to dispose of the nations supply of Nerve gas. The atoll was very small and had just enough room for the airplane to land. We were on the atoll for about 45 minutes unloading cargo and then we left and continued our island hopping adventure stopping at Majuro, Kwajalein, and

Kosrae. We were allowed to get off the plane on Majuro where there was a small shop where you could purchase hand made baskets. We were on Majuro for about an hour. Finally we got to Pohnpei where Len Newell and Ed Petties met us. We checked into our hotel which wasn't much. It was comprised of small rooms that were located above a small trading post. We got a very small room with a window air conditioner that sounded like a B52 bomber when you turned it on. It was hot enough in that room that you needed to leave the air conditioner running most of the time.

Pohnpei

The next day, we were taken to a small island Nan Mado. Getting to the island was no easy task. We got on a small skiff for the trip across a very beautiful reef. Here, the water was so clear, that you hardly knew that you were floating on water. Once on the island, I noticed the series of canals that were lined with long black logs along the canals and the banks of the small islands that make up this sacred place. When you ask the natives how all this got there, they would respond that it was magic. The rock logs that lined the canals did not appear to come from the local area and I believe that it is still a mystery as to where this material came from. Nan Mado is often called the Venice of the Pacific. It used to be the ceremonial and political seat of the Saudeleur dynasty that united Pohnpei's estimated 25,000 people from about AD 500 until 1500, when the centralized system collapsed.

Following or visit to Nan Mado, we returned to Pohnpei, where the island natives put on a feast for us. This was followed by speeches from the natives and our guide Len Newell. The following day, we got on with the business at hand. The communications system on the island was almost nonexistent. In emergencies simple radio systems were used for search and rescue operations. Telephone was available but you had to go to a central place and have an operator place the call for you. Overall there was not too much I could do to improve the communications system on this island. We did uncover a major problem, namely one of the groups from the United Nations was trying to introduce goats to the island. This could be a disaster as goats can literally damage the landscape and foliage. We went to the US Embassy and expressed our concerns.

We moved on and flew to Truk. Truk is the place in the Pacific where we caught up with the Japanese Navy and sunk over 100 of their ships. The Truk Lagoon is a favorite place of scuba divers to visit. Major problems on this island as with other islands in the Pacific is the lack of water. On Truk, there is water rationing and during the day, the water is turned off for most of the daylight hours. The other thing is that the electricity is not too reliable and the power is constantly going off and on.

Xavier High School

We visited Xavier High School. This is a place where the upcoming leaders from Micronesia come to advance their education. The school is located in an old Japanese radio station which had been heavily fortified during World War II. The shutters and outside doors were made of steel and were about 12 inches thick. The roof of the structure was pitted from the numerous bombings during the war. Electrical power was from a windmill and was supplemented with gasoline driven generators. The student's accommodations were a cement floor where they would put down their grass mats to sleep.

After a couple of days we moved on to Guam. This is the island that I was able to assist with their communications problems. Guam has a lot of what we would call forest fires. The fires are set by the natives because they like to hunt and have found that hunting is easier when you have large clearings that have been created by fire. The other agency on the island that was having communications problems was the Fish and Wildlife service. Both Forestry and the Fish and Wild Life Service have very old communications systems and often during fires radio communications would be lost. I started the wheels turning and called back to my office and got a couple of engineers looking at the Guam topography to see if we could build a good modern communications system on that island. The answer came back that yes it was feasible and would not be too expensive. I started the ball rolling to get financing for this project and I hoped to come back for the dedication of the new radio station. Little did I know at the time that I would never be able to return.

Saipan The Last Command

We moved on to Saipan, Rota, and were able to observe the remnants from the war. There were leftover reminders such as old pill boxes, the memorials where hundreds of Japanese had committed suicide. The place where the Japanese made their last stand was also memorialized. The bunker and old cannon are still there. I remember thinking to myself about what a hell it must have been to invade these islands in all that heat and humidity, carrying all the necessary equipment to make the invasion successful.

While on Rota, we came across a problem where it became apparent that for whatever reason, the island government had not been reimbursed for some of its expenses related to the islands re vegetation project. I contacted the Regional fiscal agent to find out what the problem was. Payment was 18 months overdue. There was no good explanation and I got the ball rolling to get the island government paid.

Rota was an interesting island in that the small town that we stayed in had loud speakers mounted all over town. During the middle of the day, music was played for everyone who was in town. The other interesting thing about Rota was that it was the only island where you could drink the water right from the tap. This was because the water supply was filtered through a natural limestone cave. Following the war, the Army Corps of Engineers ran a pipeline down to the town from the cave, giving the community good clean fresh water to drink. Len and Ed decided to show me the cave and I didn't have any idea what was in store for me. The cave was a relatively short hike through an overgrown area. It was very hot and humid on the day that we picked to hike up to the cave. I made it about ¾ of the way and the heat and humidity started getting to me. I had to rest every few steps. I finally made it to the cave and proceeded to try and drink all the water that was in the cave. Going back down was a lot easier. When I got back to our room, I removed everything that I had been wearing. My shirt pants and shoes had the most horrible smell. It was off to the Laundromat.

The last island that we visited was Yap. Yap is unique from the standpoint that their money is round stones with hole in the center. We visited the Bechiyal Village. To get there we hiked down a narrow path for a couple of miles. Once in the village, we were greeted by a couple of local villagers. We were given a fresh coconut for refreshment and were taken to a building called the "Man's House". This is a place where the village men go and stay the night before they go out fishing.

We returned to Guam and boarded an all night flight back to Honolulu. In Honolulu, I spent a couple of days working with the folks from the experiment station. After 6 weeks we flew home and I returned to work. My number 1 project was to get that radio station built on Guam. To do this, I recruited the lead electronic technician from the Los Padres National Forest. The hardest part of recruiting was to convince him that he needed a passport. Even though Guam is a US territory, one needs a passport to go there. I also worked on getting funding to purchase the equipment necessary for the radio station. Part of the project included purchase of a prefabricated building that would be airlifted to the top of one of the mountain peaks. The radio station would get completed in the spring of 1988 and I was looking forward to going back for the dedication ceremony. Little did I know that I would no longer be in the Forest Service when the dedication took place.

By the mid 1980's the Consent Decree that had been entered into while I was in the Washington Office was beginning to heat up and give many Regional managers problems in recruiting. The decree had started as a complaint filed by a lady who worked at the experiment station in Berkley. It was a good example of a situation that could have been avoided if the Station's personnel office had done its job. When the complaint was originally filed, the Forest Service had requested that the case be tried in Federal court. A decision was made by the Department of Justice to enter into a consent decree. The Forest Service objected to this but the Justice Department had the final say. The Decree would set targets for the Forest Service to meet. The targets were intended to give women better opportunities for career advancement within the Forest Service. Even though the original complaint had originated in the experiment station, the final decree included both the Experiment Station and Region 5.

At first, the Forest Service moved pretty slowly in implementing the decree. This was new uncharted territory for the agency. As time progressed and there were only marginal changes visible, more and more intervention took place requiring the Forest Service to hire and promote more women. The backlash was that men who had been in the agency for over 20 years suddenly found themselves in a position where it was difficult to advance ones career. I remember being put on a panel that put together a promotion roster for a Regional airplane pilot. The roster would have several names on it including the name of the flying mechanic who had been a good friend and mentor of mine when I first started working for the Forest Service at the Chino airport. I remember being shocked when we were told that there was no way that a man could be selected for this position. This seemed quite unfair to me. The person who I had known at Chino had given a lot to the Forest Service and had been required to spend long periods of time away from his family during the Fire Season.

A frustration that I had with the decree was that even when I tried to fill one of my Branch Chief positions with a highly qualified woman, I got very strong resistance from the Regional Personnel Officer. This was amazing to me as the Regional Personnel Officer was a lady that had been recruited from another agency to fill the Personnel Officers job. I finally was able to get the person that I wanted and she turned out to be a great asset to my organization. By the mid 1980's, my staff would be ranked one of the highest in the Forest Service for having women managers and minorities. By the late 1980's my management team would be comprised of 66% women. My overall staff would be 51% minority with many of the minority personnel and women in journeyman level positions. To accomplish this, I had setup upward mobility positions when I had first arrived in the Region and I had deliberately recruited women into these positions. The Region however as a whole was not doing very well. Things would get a lot worse as time progressed.

Being a Director meant that your were expected to conduct management reviews in your area of expertise. The reviews took place on the Regions National Forest. You were also expected to accompany the Regional Forester or deputy Regional Forester on program reviews on the ground in the National Forest. I accompanied our Regional Forester, Zane Smith on a review of the Inyo National Forest. I was quite familiar with this Forest as I had visited it several times when I was growing up. This was also the Forest where we had been based when I was working on Project Flambeau. I thought I knew everything there was to know about the Inyo Forest until I went there with Zane. During our review, we were taken to the White Mountain Range which is home to a stand of Bristle Cone Pines. What is interesting about these trees is that they are perhaps the oldest living things on earth. It is estimated that some of these trees are over 4000 years old. The other thing is that unlike humans, the Bristle Cone Pine seems to do extremely well in growth areas where the tree is stressed due to climate and growing conditions.

On another review of the San Bernardino National Forest, I accompanied my boss Deputy Regional Forester Warren Davies on a horseback trip through part of the Morongo Valley. This was an experience as I had not been on a horse since my early 20s. The night before the trip we had a barbeque at a small camp site. There were a lot of different kinds of food available but the one I remember most was the prairie sidewinder (rattle snake). The next day began with us catching our horses and saddling them up. My mother had made sure when I was growing up that I got horseback riding lessons and as a kid I had learned how to handle horses and put the saddle on them. I am sure my boss was impressed as he let me and one of the other members of the team catch his horse. The ride through the valley was interesting but towards the end I realized that I was getting very sore. You may have heard the old saying that people who take long horse back rides have to eat their dinner from the mantle. By the end of the ride, I really needed a mantle. After the ride we drove down to Palm Springs. I watched as the other folks on the team soaked themselves in the motels hot tub. I hadn't brought a swim suit so I was out of luck in this department.

As a Director, I made it a point to visit each National Forest in the Region at least once a year. This in its self was a large task as the Region had 17 National Forest and the Lake Tahoe Management Unit. The job was made easier as I had access to the Regions fleet of Beach Barron aircraft. We called the Regions fleet Bear Air. It was truly a luxury to be able to call the dispatcher and arrange to have the Barron pick me up at the Concord Buchanan airport. My visits to the Forest were greatly appreciated by the Forest Supervisors. One of their biggest complaints was that Directors sat in the Regional Office, never came out to the Forest and were totally unaware of what the real problems were on the ground.

The management reviews were interesting as they covered more than just my area of expertise. On a review on the Inyo National Forest we visited the Mammoth Ski Resort. Here there are many ski lifts on land that the Forest Service leases to the lift operators. The Mammoth ski resort was started by a person who early in life had done surveys of the snow pack in the Mammoth Lakes area. He got the idea of providing a simple rope tow for would be skiers. By the mid 1980s this person was a multi millionaire and the Mammoth ski resort had become one of the largest ski resorts in California. We had occasion to take one of the lifts up the mountain to inspect one of our radio repeaters that was located near the top of the lift. While there we got a tour of the lift facility and were able to look at the equipment that the lift operator used for making ski movies and safety films.

Communications is a vital part of the Inyo Forest Safety program. The Forest is located on top of an old volcano and during the 1980s there was real concern that the volcano could erupt. At one point during the 80s, seismic activity increased to the point where there were earthquakes almost every day. Magma was detected rising to within 100 feet of the surface near the highway intersection of Interstate I 395 and the Mammoth Lakes turnoff. The heat from the magma was so intense that it was killing some of the nearby vegetation. The concern was so great for the safety of the Mammoth residents that the Forest Service Engineers built an escape road for the residents. This was to be used in the event of an eruption. From the communication side, a major telephone cable ran through the area and if there was an eruption, telephone communications covering a very large area would be cut off. The other problem was that in the event of an eruption, there would be so much interference that normal radio communications would also be cut off. My communications experts studied the problem and found out at that time, some types of Ham radio systems would work.

On another review on the Klamath National Forest, we observed the dredging operations along the Klamath river. There were portions of the river that had so much equipment that the beauty of the river had been ruined. We were traveling along the river in route to one of the Forest Districts where the Forest Supervisor had ask us to evaluate the District computer operator. The operator did not seem to be following Forest Service procedures and there was a concern that the District computer operations might be compromised. We decided to make a rest stop at a scenic rest stop. There was a small waterfall there and it was a great place to take a break. We pulled the van over an got out. No sooner had we left the van, I heard what sounded like a fire arm being cocked. I glanced towards the sound and sure enough a group of people who had proceeded us to the rest area were one by one cocking their weapons. We got in the van and left. There was no way to report the incident as the van did not have a radio and in the mid 1980s cell phones were not very common. We reported the incident when we got to the ranger station.

While at the District, we did a thorough review of the Districts computer operations and we concluded that procedures were not being followed. We also noticed that the District operator seemed to have an attitude problem and was almost antagonistic to the review team. After we left the District we worked with the Ranger and the Forest Computer Specialist to develop a strategy for removing the District computer operator and at the same time safeguard the information that was on the District computer system.

By the mid 1980s, things began to change in the Forest Service Information Technology area. My old Boss Glenn Haney was transferred to head up the Department of Agriculture's Information Processing Office. He was replaced by a controversial individual who some folks thought that he had been promoted into a position so that he could do no more harm to the agency. Other people thought that this person was doing a great job and that he had received a merit promotion. The one thing that I knew about him was that he had a very strong dislike for those of us who had worked for Hobby Bonnet. I remember one Forest Supervisor saying that it was really sad to see a person who had such a bad track record get promoted into an Associate Deputy Chief's position. The director of Computer Science, Jack Arthur left the Forest Service for a position in the Department of Interior and he was replaced by Clyde Shumway. Several years later, Jack would return to the Forest Service where he would remain for the rest of his career. Soon after Clyde became Director, other changes were made. The IT Director from Region 3 was given a directed reassignment to Washington DC. His comments to his friends were that he had been put in a corner and wasn't given anything to do. He was replaced by a person who knew almost nothing about information processing. Work at the Forest Service Systems Applications group in Ft. Collins was getting reassigned to the Systems group in Region 1. There were very strong ties between Region 1 and the new Associate Deputy Chief. The unit at Ft. Collins was disbanded and the technical staff there was transferred to new locations. This was very expensive for the tax payers. The Head of this group was demoted and would remain for a short time as the Forest Service Liaison with the Ft. Collins Computer Center. He would soon retire and the position would be abolished. This was payback for helping the Forest Service establish a productive computer shop in Region 1, Missoula Montana, volunteering to help establish the Forest Service Payment Center in Ft. Collins, transferring to Washington DC to help establish the new Computer Science Organizations and then transferring back to Ft. Collins. I guess his only mistake was that he had worked for Hobby Bonnet and the new Associate Deputy didn't care for anyone who had worked for Hobby. Still another work associate of mine wanted to transfer back home to the Atlanta area where he had come from several years earlier. He had worked many years in Washington and had been the Director of Computer Science in Region 3 for a couple of years. When he applied for the opening in Atlanta, the Associate Deputy Chief told him that no way would he ever be considered for the Directors position in Atlanta. This individual would leave the Forest Service and would work for Glenn Haney in the Department's Data Communications group. Mike Slimp who had worked for me in Region 5, and had worked in the Washington Office took the Directors position in Region 4. After a couple of years Mike got so frustrated that he resigned and went into business for himself.

I watched all this from Region 5 and thought what a shame it was that all these people who had given so much to the outfit were now resigning, retiring, or being forced into taking an unwanted transfer. I was not concerned with my own job as I had great performance ratings an excellent rapport with the Forest Service Engineering and Fire Management organizations. I had a done lot to help these groups out. In the case of Engineering, I had championed their cause for the purchase and maintenance of Personal Computers (PCs) and

I had helped the Regional Fire Management group with adapting some of their applications to PCs. I also maintained a great working relationship with different factions in the Department of Agriculture. People from other Regions and the Department became regulars at Region 5 meetings and workshops. Even with bad things happening to some of my associates, I was at the height of my career and really enjoying my job.

In 1987, the Chief of the Forest Service made a visit to the Region and shortly after the morning briefing all personnel in the Regional Office were told to go to a local theater down the street at 10:00AM. There was going to be a major announcement. The announcement was that Zane Smith the Regional Forester was being replaced. The new Regional Forester would be Paul Barker. Zane and I did not always see eye to eye but Zane had been a good hard working person who had served the Forest Service well. Zane would be allowed to work for a few months on a special project for the Chief's office and then he would retire. This was a shock to the Region but we all knew that the reason for Zane's removal was that the Region was not meeting the goals set by the Regional Consent Decree.

In the fall of 1987, I was dispatched to a major fire in Region 6. The request was that I bring a couple of experienced people with me who knew how to use personal computers (PCs). One of my Branch Chiefs Libby Hecker would accompany me along with my lead computer Specialist Don Mc Coy. Getting to the fire was half the fun. We would fly to Portland on Air California and then go to the general aviation terminal and wait for a Forest Service contract plane to pick us up. We had brought 3 PCs with us which were quite awkward to transport. Computer Laptops were just coming into being and were not readily available. The contract plane picked us up and flew us to the La Grande Complex in La Grande OR. The Main fire camp was located on the campus of a Community College and we checked in with the Fire Time keeper. We spent that night sleeping on the lawn in paper sleeping bags. Other than the fact that the paper sleeping bags don't last very long, they are pretty comfortable. In the morning, I went to the morning briefing and learned the current status of the fire. We then began to set up shop, using our PCs and simple spreadsheet programs to solve some of the bookkeeping problems associated with the management of large fire management projects. In the 1980s much of the fire management was done using paper and pencil. There was a Forest Level Data General computer located in La Grande but is was small and was dedicated to just getting the Forest daily computer traffic processed.

On the 3rd day that we worked the fire, Clyde Shumway showed up and walked through our area. He smiled and said hi and left right away. My sources told me later that Clyde was furious that I had brought PCs to the fire. After several days we returned to our office feeling that our project had been quite successful.

As 1987 came to a close, I got my performance rating. As usual it was exceptional. The part of my review that concerned me was that my boss informed me that the classification of my position was being changed from a Computer Systems Administrator to a Management Analyst. The standard for IT Staff Directors at that time was Computer Systems Administrators or a Computer Specialist and in rare cases a Computer Scientist. What concerned me was that changing the classification would enable just about anyone with general qualifications to be the IT Director in Region 5. Computer Systems Administrators and Computer Specialist had specific requirements and qualifications that were required for a person to hold the position. Even with my protest, my job was reclassified.

In January of 1988, the Washington Office contacted me and ask if I would host the upcoming Regional IT Directors meeting. The meeting was scheduled for mid March. I asked the Washington Office contact if the Washington Office would help pay for a guest speaker at the National meeting. A few days later I got the answer. The Washington Office would put up the money for the speaker. I was also told that Clyde Shumway was very unhappy about funding the speaker. I reminded my contact of the many times when I was in the Washington Office that I had fully funded Clyde Shumway's projects. One last thing that I did was schedule the Regional Forester Paul Barker to give a welcome speach to the group attending the meeting. In sending out the invitations to the meeting, I ask for people to indicate if they would attend the evening banquet where our guest speaker would give his speech on management and management practices. The response was incredible. We got responses from over 100 people. As usual several people from the Department of Agriculture invited themselves to our meeting.

The meeting date finally came and Paul Barkers speech was well received. This was a first as nobody prior to that meeting had ever invited a Regional Forester to kickoff an IT Directors meeting. The meeting progressed well and it was nearing time for our dinner and guest speaker. I was passing time at the bar with an old friend from USDA at the bar. We had a couple of hours before the dinner was scheduled to start. During the conversation, I was asked if I was aware that a contracting officer, Clyde Thompson, from the Forest Service Washington Office, was telling everyone in the Washington Office and the Department that he would soon be coming to San

Francisco to take my job. At first I shrugged these comments off as being ridicules. As the discussion progressed, my friend told me that the way that Clyde was going to get my job was that his wife's specialty was in program planning and budgeting (PPB). That comment caught my attention and it all came together. Clyde's wife would take the vacant Branch Chief's position in PPB. In order to place her, they would have to find a job for Clyde. They couldn't put him in as the Contracts Director as that position had just been filled. It would be very easy to slip Clyde into my job as the position classification had been modified and there were no specialty requirements associated with it. This would give the Region double hero points as Clyde and his wife were both minorities plus the benefit of placing a woman in a high level position would help meet the consent decree goals. Needless to say, my blood ran cold and I knew that my days in Region 5 were coming to an end.

As time went on, I began getting more warnings from my close friends and allies in the Department and Washington Office Forest Service. People working in Clyde Shumway's office were intercepting letters on the staff printer. These letters were discussing my fate and the placement of Clyde Thompson into my position. Copies of these letters were sent to me with the hope that the letters would help me in a potential lawsuit against the Forest Service.

I began looking at my options, and I was still kind of in shock, wondering how an outfit that I had spent nearly 30 years of my life with, could sacrifice me in order to meet an artificial target? This was like having a bad dream. The options that I began looking into included:

Early retirement. In the 1980s if you had worked for the Federal government for more than 25 years and were given a directed reassignment against your will, you could retire instead of taking the new assignment. This would cost you in terms of penalties you pay, namely a reduction in your monthly annuity.

I could file a grievance. There was little doubt in my mind that I could prove that the Forest Service had violated my civil service rights and that I would prevail and keep my job. The problem with this was that if I remained in my position, the Forest Service could retaliate and give me poor performance ratings and then remove me from office. If this happened, I would be out of a job and would not be able to collect my pension until age 65.

I could confront the Regional Forester with the information that I had and throw a monkey wrench into the Forest Service plans before the plans were set in concrete. This alternative could have the same consequences as in the 2nd alternative.

April came and went and I was beginning to wonder if this whole thing had been a bad dream. I visited with the Regional HR Director, Tom Brown, and asked him point blank if there was something going on to place Clyde Thompson in my job and give me a directed reassignment. Tom just laughed the whole thing off and told me that there was no way the Washington Office could pull this off. He also told me that if this was in the works, he would surely know about it and he said he hadn't heard a thing. I decided to let the issue drop. By mid May, I was beginning to feel a little bit better and I began to believe that for what ever reason the Chief's Office had changed its mind. We had a great Labor day weekend and returned to our 7:30AM briefing on Tuesday morning. As the meeting was wrapping up, the Regional Forester, Paul Barker invited the Land Management Planning (LMP) Director to meet with him immediately following the briefing. He also told me to give him about 20 minutes and then for me to stop by his office. I left the morning briefing and I knew it was all over for me. My worst dream was about to come true.

I reported the Regional Foresters Office about 20 minutes later. Paul began speaking and it only took a few words for him to tell me that I was being moved to the Washington Office. He went a little bit further by telling me that he thought that a tour in the Washington Office would be great for me and good for the Forest Service. I had known Paul when I worked in Washington so I thought that he was just being very nice or had just forgotten that I had already done a nine year tour in Washington DC. I responded to Paul, telling him thanks for the offer but that I would be retiring effective July 1. That took Paul completely by surprise. I am sure that he didn't know that I had had a lot of advance warning and had time to think about all of my options.

Following my meeting with the Regional Forester, I returned to my office. I told my secretary to notify the staff that there would be a 10:00 AM staff meeting. I remember going into my office and taking several minutes to regain my composure. This whole thing really hurt. At 10:00 AM I went to my staff meeting and let my staff of about 40 people know that I had been given a directed reassignment and that I would be retiring effective July 1. I then took leave for the rest of the day and went home.

During the few weeks that followed, several people in the Washington Office visited with their respective Deputy Chiefs and pleaded my case. They made a valiant effort to get the Chief's decision reversed.

In the Regional Office, the 3 Directors who knew my plight went to the Regional Forester and strongly suggested that he intervene in my behalf. None of this did any good and my fate was set.

On the day before my last day in the Forest Service, Paul Barker announced at the morning briefing that I was retiring rather than accepting a transfer to the Washington Office. The other staff Directors who hadn't heard about what was going on were shocked. Following the briefing most of the Directors came to my office to talk to me and try to figure out what had happened. Some of them actually had tears in their eyes. I told them all what had transpired. Several of them were very concerned that If this had happened to me, it could happen to them as well. This whole thing would have lasting effects on the Region.

On my last day in the Forest Service, my wife suggested that I just take the day off and not bother to go to work. She knew that this day was going to be very hard on me. I left the house and took the Vallejo ferry to San Francisco. The Directors had a small farewell party for me and they had delayed the meeting so that I could take the ferry to work. Following my party and the morning briefing, I took a large brown envelope to the Regional Foresters Office. The envelope contained a formal complaint that simply stated that I thought I had been discriminated against. The complaint would stop all attempts by the Forest Service to fill my old job position. Complaints of this type are very carefully reviewed by the Department of Agriculture and there was a possibility that the Civil Service commission could get involved. Within days of my retirement, I would be assigned a representative from a different Region to represent me in my case. The case would drag out for six to eight months. In the interim, the Region would give my old Branch Chief Margy Nickelson a temporary promotion into my old position. This would be an excellent opportunity for Margy to gain experience in a top level management position. Other than the brief farewell party, the day was very uneventful. I would receive about 100+ emails from people service wide who would wish me well and thank me for helping them out over the years. Things were so slow that by mid day I took a short nap in my office then went out to lunch with a couple of close friends. At the end of the day I signed my final pay slip and left a few minutes early. I walked down to the ferry building to catch my ride home.

Epilogue:
Life outside the Forest Service

I had envisioned starting a small business when I retired. I made a run at it but found that this was more difficult than I had imagined. Years later, I would successfully start and run a small business. This would keep me busy into my 70s. I would eventually drop my complaint against the Forest Service. I did this as it was becoming apparent to me that there was a good chance that I would win. Had I won the case, I would have been reinstated with all my back pay. My concern was if I got my job back, there would be a backlash by the Forest Service and I would eventually get fired and end up losing all of my benefits. I would work for a short time for a local newspaper, contract for doing a study for the state of California and work for a defense contractor on Mare Island. Here I would become very proficient in technical writing. Specifically, I would write "how to manuals" for the Navy. After about 4 years the Navy would close Mare Island and I would go to work for another contractor. The new company that I worked for, ATA managed government IT facilities doing everything from data entry, computer operations and systems engineering. I worked for this company for about four months and was promoted to the Area Managers position. My area covered Northern California and Nevada. I had the responsibility for 150 plus IT professionals and my Area brought in a very large revenue for the company. A few years later, I moved on and joined a new company and provided Technical

Support to the company's clients. This job would ultimately help me set up my small business of providing Technical Support to computer users in the Home Inspection Business. The last significant job that I would hold would be working in the Computer Gaming Industry. Here I would test new software and work with program developers to fix bugs in the programs.

It's been over 21 years since I retired from the Forest Service. I still wakeup at night having had a bad dream about what had happened to me and the way I left the agency. I still have a hard time believing that the Forest Service had sacrificed me. One of the interesting things that I observed when I was working for ATA was that I would run into some of the women who I had recruited into my Forest Service Staff and had trained. Within a fairly short time following my retirement, these women would leave the Forest Service and work for different government agencies. I guess in the long run, the Forest Service was able to displace me so that they could put a woman in a branch chief job and give her husband my job. In the long run, the Forest Service would be the loser.

CPSIA information can be obtained at www.ICGtesting.com
Printed in the USA
BVOW021642071111

275503BV00001B/61/P